THE GLORIOUS REVOLUTION

The Glorious Revolution
SECOND EDITION

JOHN MILLER

Routledge
Taylor & Francis Group

LONDON AND NEW YORK

First published 1983 by Pearson Education Limited
Second Edition 1997

This edition published 2014 by Routledge
2 Park Square, Milton Park, Abingdon, Oxon OX14 4RN
711 Third Avenue, New York, NY 10017, USA

Routledge is an imprint of the Taylor & Francis Group, an informa business

Copyright © 1983, 1997, Taylor & Francis

The right of John Miller to be identified as author
of this Work has been asserted by him in accordance
with the Copyright, Designs and Patents Act 1988.

Notices
Knowledge and best practice in this field are constantly changing. As new research and
experience broaden our understanding, changes in research methods, professional
practices, or medical treatment may become necessary.

Practitioners and researchers must always rely on their own experience and knowledge
in evaluating and using any information, methods, compounds, or experiments
described herein. In using such information or methods they should be mindful of
their own safety and the safety of others, including parties for whom they have a
professional responsibility.

To the fullest extent of the law, neither the Publisher nor the authors, contributors, or
editors, assume any liability for any injury and/or damage to persons or property as a
matter of products liability, negligence or otherwise, or from any use or operation of
any methods, products, instructions, or ideas contained in the material herein.

ISBN 13: 978-0-582-29222-2 (pbk)

British Library Cataloguing in Publication Data

A catalogue record for this book is available from the British Library

Library of Congress Cataloging-in-Publication Data

Miller, John, 1946–
   The glorious revolution / John Miller. -- 2nd ed.
      p.   cm. -- (Seminar studies in history)
   Includes bibliographical references and index.
   ISBN 0-582-29222-0
   1. Great Britain--History--Revolution of 1688. I. Title.
II. Series.
DA452.M55 1997
941.06'7--dc21
                                                          96-51472
                                                             CIP

CONTENTS

AN INTRODUCTION TO THE SERIES

Such is the pace of historical enquiry in the modern world that there is an ever-widening gap between the specialist article or monograph, incorporating the results of current research, and general surveys, which inevitably become out of date. *Seminar Studies in History* are designed to bridge this gap. The series was founded by Patrick Richardson in 1966 and his aim was to cover major themes in British, European and World history. Between 1980 and 1996 Roger Lockyer continued his work, before handing the editorship over to Clive Emsley and Gordon Martel. Clive Emsley is Professor of History at the Open University, while Gordon Martel is Professor of International History at the University of Northern British Columbia, Canada and Senior Research Fellow at De Montfort University.

All the books are written by experts in their field who are not only familiar with the latest research but have often contributed to it. They are frequently revised, in order to take account of new information and interpretations. They provide a selection of documents to illustrate major themes and provoke discussion, and also a guide to further reading. The aim of *Seminar Studies* is to clarify complex issues without over-simplifying them, and to stimulate readers into deepening their knowledge and understanding of major themes and topics.

NOTE ON REFERENCING SYSTEM

Readers should note that numbers in square brackets [5] refer them to the corresponding entry in the Bibliography at the end of the book (specific page numbers are given in italics). A number in square brackets preceded by *Doc.* [*Doc.* 5] refers readers to the corresponding item in the Documents section which follows the main text.

PREFACE

To most Englishmen of the eighteenth and nineteenth centuries the Revolution of 1688–9 was indeed 'glorious'. It thwarted James II's attempt to establish a Catholic absolutism and made possible the continuation and extension of parliamentary government and the rule of law. This view received its most magisterial statement from Lord Macaulay, who saw in the Revolution the seeds of every good and liberal law enacted in the next century and a half [90]. The 'Whig' or liberal values of Macaulay continued to influence historians. 'The Revolution', wrote Trevelyan, 'gave to England an ordered and legal freedom and through that it gave her power' [138 p. 240]. To David Ogg, who compared absolutism to fascism, the Revolution played a vital role in the formation of Anglo-Saxon civilisation 'maintained by communities which are as ready to defend their liberties as they are unwilling to enforce them on others' [101 p. 547]. The legacy of the Revolution was, indeed, not confined to England. One has only to read the United States constitution to see strong signs of the influence of the Revolution and of its greatest apologist, John Locke.

The tercentenary of the Revolution, in 1988, stimulated an attempt to reassess its importance. There were several exhibitions and numerous conferences, whose proceedings have since been published. Most of these sought to consider the Revolution in the widest possible context, which had the curious effect of taking the central events – and their constitutional significance – for granted. Meanwhile, the importance (and gloriousness) of the Revolution was questioned in Parliament, the press and elsewhere. Some denounced the celebration of an event whose *raison d'être* was anti-Catholic. Those who dismissed the Revolution as unimportant came from opposite ends of the political spectrum, but their conclusions were broadly similar.

From the Left came the assertion that the Revolution was insignificant, a mere palace putsch, because the real 'English revolution' had already taken place in 1640–60. Whereas in those years the old social and political order had been turned upside-down, 1688 merely reinforced the dominance of the propertied over the propertyless. The very terms of this argument call into question the permanence of the impact of the earlier revolution; it also presupposes that the causes of the civil war were essentially socio-economic, a view that recent research has called seriously into question.

An alternative argument, which also reduced the Revolution to a dynastic *coup*, was that 1688 changed nothing and England's 'ancien regime' continued essentially unchanged until 1828–32. Such arguments rest heavily on the relatively conventional provisions of the Bill of Rights and a view of eighteenth-century society which emphasises deference, Anglicanism and the countryside as against conflict, Dissent (or indifference) and the towns (especially London) [26; 40; 41]. The stress on the change of dynasty is linked to a strong assertion of the strength and importance of Jacobitism, a point on which historians have widely differing views [47; 97]. This led to such bizarre phenomena as a newspaper article dividing the Convention of 1689 into Whigs and Jacobites: strange indeed to find the *Sunday Telegraph* writing the Tory party out of history.

These attempts to deny or belittle the importance of the Revolution have been vigorously rebuffed by historians, although without the element of moralising, the conviction that it was a 'good thing', which one finds in Macaulay, Trevelyan and Ogg. Most agree that the Revolution led to major changes. The two long wars of the English succession, between 1689 and 1713, led England to develop a European and world role out of all proportion to her population and resources. Recent work on the growth of the 'fiscal-military state', and the extension of earlier work on the 'financial revolution', have shown how the Revolution led to a transformation of the English state – albeit one that built on the changes of the 1640s [31; 33; 52; 80; 108]. Research on eighteenth-century religion has shown that to depict English society as 'Anglican' is simplistic and misleading [78; 125; 126]. Nor was it static. Economic historians stress the emergence of a consumer society, embracing the relatively humble as well as the rich, in which fashion and taste were becoming more important than functionality. Manners and style became increasingly important within what came to be known as 'polite' society [30; 92]. The juxtaposition of the old and the new bred friction and occasionally conflict, seen in economic disputes, riots and party political divisions. After the news explosion of the 1640s, politics could never again be the preserve of a smallish elite. With the growth of the provincial press in the eighteenth century, the English public became one of the best-informed in Europe. By the 1730s, some sections of it were becoming increasingly impatient with the Walpolean political system [51; 89; 104; 128].

If recent research has not (I think) radically changed our understanding of the events of the Revolution, or of its constitutional significance, it has certainly changed our understanding of post-Revolution government and society. It has also stressed how anglocentric the (English) Whig view was. The official celebrations of the tercentenary barely mentioned Scotland and ignored Ireland – not surprisingly, perhaps, in view of the troubles, but the result was inevitably an incomplete picture. The first edition of this book was justifiably criticised for dealing with them cursorily. Since it was written, historians have become much more aware of the 'British' context of England's history and the interactions between England, Scotland and Ireland [32]. This second edition includes a fuller discussion of Scotland and Ireland, which serves, I believe, to reinforce the central contention of the first – that the Revolution had a major impact on subsequent British history. Whether that impact was good or bad is for the reader to decide.

JOHN MILLER

PART ONE: THE BACKGROUND

1   THE FALL OF JAMES II

When James, Duke of York, was proclaimed king on 6 February 1685, few would have predicted that within four years he would be in exile in France, his departure regretted by few of his subjects. Although the ports were closed and guards patrolled London's streets, there was no disorder and many expressed joy at the new king's accession.

The ease of his accession came as a surprise. A few years before, there had been a concerted attempt to exclude him from the succession to his brother's throne on the grounds that he was a Catholic. Three times between 1679 and 1681 the Commons had passed exclusion bills, but the Lords rejected one and the others were frustrated by Charles's dismissing Parliament. The Exclusion Crisis marked the climax of a growing mistrust between Charles and his parliaments. Parliament had welcomed Charles back in 1660 and had taken care to restore an effective monarchy, to guard against any recurrence of the upheavals of the civil wars and Interregnum, but in return had expected Charles to rule more responsibly than his father had done in the 1630s. Trust in the king was badly shaken by his alliance with the Catholic and absolutist Louis XIV, who was generally believed to be seeking to establish a universal monarchy. MPs also expressed anxiety about the 'growth of Popery' at home, partly because of Charles's attempt to grant Catholics a modest toleration in 1672, but more because James, his heir presumptive, had become a Catholic.

In 1678 Titus Oates revealed an alleged 'Popish Plot' to assassinate Charles. Although his story was a pack of lies, few doubted its veracity and its implications were alarming. Hitherto the prospect of a Catholic king, although worrying, had been far from immediate. Charles was only three years older than James and in excellent health. If, as seemed likely, he outlived James, he would be succeeded by James's elder daughter Mary – and Mary and her husband, William of Orange, were Protestants. Oates's story forced people to consider what would have happened had Charles been killed. Experience taught that Catholic rulers persecuted their Protestant subjects with implacable cruelty, ignoring the constraints of humanity, morality and law. Catholic rule was identified with violence, armed force and illegality – in short, 'arbitrary government' [*Doc. 1*] like that of Louis XIV. Although Oates declared that James was not involved in the plot, he was its obvious beneficiary. To save themselves from absolutism and bloody persecution it seemed to a majority of the Commons and the electorate that it was essential, a matter of self-preservation, to exclude James from the succession.

The exclusion campaign was the logical culmination of the Commons' growing distrust of both James and Charles. The outcome was less predictable. Charles would not agree to exclusion, which he saw as part of a broader attack on the rights and powers of the Crown. In their efforts to overcome his resistance, the Exclusionists (or 'Whigs') challenged his essential prerogatives (for example, his right to call and dismiss parliaments) and mobilised mass support, using techniques of agitation and propaganda reminiscent of those used in 1641–2. As the panic of the plot died down, many who had been unhappy about Charles and James's conduct in the 1670s came to see in the Whigs' tactics a greater threat to the established order in Church and state than anything that James might do; more and more conservatives ('tories') rallied to the defence of 'Church and king'. They wished to maintain the ascendancy of the Church of England, against both Catholics and Protestant Dissenters, and to support the monarchy against the apparent threat of civil war.

The Tories' opposition to exclusion led the Whigs to denounce them as 'Papists in disguise'. The mutual recriminations of Whig and Tory had, by 1681, divided the ruling elite more deeply than at any time since 1660. Charles eagerly exploited this division, throwing the full weight of his authority behind the Tories. He dismissed Whigs from offices in local government and the militia and put Tories in their places. He encouraged the persecution of Dissenters, most of whom had supported Exclusion. Above all, he used the law courts as instruments of political vengeance. Whigs prosecuted on charges of treason or on private suits were condemned by Tory judges and Tory juries. The king could not change the magistrates of the towns, most of which had charters allowing them to choose their own; in many cases these were Dissenters, or Whigs, who failed to enforce the laws against Dissent. Local Tories and the central government co-operated in having these charters surrendered or quashed. New ones were issued which gave the king the power to remove officials and members of the corporation at will, giving the Crown greater control than ever before over the boroughs' internal affairs. In parliamentary boroughs, it would also be able to influence elections [93].

By 1685, a few years after the monarchy seemed to be tottering, it had broken the Whigs as a political force and was on the verge of controlling elections. However, the Crown had gained this power only with the Tories' co-operation and it could be exploited only if they continued to co-operate. Although the Whigs claimed that the Tories were unprincipled sycophants, who enlarged the king's power in return for places, the Tories had helped to build up the Crown's authority for what seemed to them sound political reasons. The Whigs, they believed, were rebels and republicans. Only a strong monarchy could prevent political and social upheaval. James's assurances that he would uphold the Church's pre-eminence, and his defence of the Episcopal Church in Scotland, made them far less apprehensive than the Whigs about the prospect of his becoming king. Even so, certain tacit conditions underlay their support for the Crown's growing authority. So long as the king protected the Church, so long as he gave the Tories a monopoly of office, so long as he bent the law only against the Whigs, the Tories were quite content. If the king tried to use his newly-acquired powers against the Tories, their reaction would be very different.

JAMES II AND HIS SUBJECTS

James had much in common with the Tories. He had an exalted view of kingly authority and expected his subjects to obey him, but he also recognised that kings had a sacred obligation to care for their subjects' welfare and to rule according to law [*Doc. 2*]. James differed from the Tories, and from the vast majority of his subjects, in being a Catholic. His conversion, in his mid-thirties, was fully considered and psychologically satisfying. He thought in terms of simple polar opposites and found in the Catholic Church an unquestionable authority, which (he felt) other Churches lacked [*Doc. 4*]. Like many converts, he wished to share his faith with others, but Catholic worship was forbidden by law and Catholics were excluded from Parliament and public office. Moreover, generations of Protestant preaching and propaganda had instilled strong prejudices against 'Popery' even if, in Defoe's words, people 'do not know whether it be a man or a horse' [*132 p. 34*].

James faced formidable obstacles in his efforts to promote Catholicism, but he was determined to try. He hoped to find a Parliament that would repeal the penal laws (which forbade Catholic worship, education and publishing) and the Test Acts (which excluded Catholics from offices and from Parliament) [*Doc. 5*]. He believed that once the Catholic clergy could compete with Protestants on equal terms, and once people could become Catholics without losing their chances of office, thousands of converts would come forward. He had no intention of imposing his religion by force: his army was predominantly Protestant and he expected to be succeeded by Mary. Not until late in 1687 was there a prospect that his queen might give birth to a son, who would take precedence over Mary and be raised as a Catholic. Until then, James assumed that Mary would succeed him and firmly rejected suggestions that he should disinherit her in favour of a Catholic [*Doc. 3*]. This meant that, in his efforts to have the penal laws and Test Acts revoked, he had to observe the forms of law, as any violence against the Protestants would be repaid, against the Catholics, after his death. As the Marquis of Halifax acutely noted:

Converts will not venture till they have such a law to secure them as hath no exception to it; so that an irregularity, or any degree of violence to the law, would so entirely take away the effect of it that men would as little run the hazard of changing their religion after the making it as before. [8 *p. 335*]

James's strategy depended on his persuading a parliament to repeal the penal laws and Test Acts. This would require the co-operation of at least a section of his subjects. England in 1685 was still a mainly agricultural country, its government and politics dominated by the landed elite, the nobility and gentry. This elite controlled most parliamentary constituencies, boroughs as well as counties, and provided the great majority of MPs. James therefore needed the co-operation of at least part of this elite to carry his programme through parliament.

Unfortunately for James, Tories and Whigs, Anglicans and Dissenters, agreed in detesting Popery, if in little else. The Tories had rallied to James in the Exclusion Crisis despite his religion, because they feared civil war. Most Tories and Whigs were against allowing Catholics freedom of worship. Those few who might allow them toleration were against their being admitted to offices or to Parliament: once in power, they believed, Catholics would persecute

Protestants. 'I can with a very good conscience', wrote the Tory Earl of Clarendon in 1688, 'give all liberty and ease to tender consciences . . . but I cannot, in conscience, give those men leave . . . to come into employments in the state who by their mistaken consciences are bound to destroy the religion I profess' [*55 p. 223*]. Although the Tories had given James the benefit of the doubt, they watched warily for signs that he might abuse his power and become another Louis XIV. Most Tories took it for granted that Catholicism and absolutism went hand in hand. James might be convinced of the purity of his intentions; he might believe that he acted only according to the law of God and the law of the land, and might dismiss his subjects' suspicions as absurd or malicious; but those suspicions, however ill-founded, were a fact of political life. Given English Protestants' preconceptions about the malign political implications of Popery, it was not surprising that James's subjects placed the worst possible construction on his conduct. James was to give them ample cause to do so.

THE COURSE OF THE REIGN

In 1685 the obvious strategy for James was to rely on his 'old friends', the Tories. He promised to maintain the Church's dominant position and continued to persecute Dissenters. This strategy was vindicated when a general election produced an overwhelmingly Tory House of Commons. This voted James the revenues enjoyed by Charles and additional sums to pay some of the Crown's debts, refit the fleet and crush the rebellion led by Charles's bastard son, the Duke of Monmouth. Monmouth's defeat seemed to signal the final destruction of Whiggery. The reprisals which followed, the Bloody Assizes, may seem abhorrent to modern eyes but aroused little protest among the Tories. The rising gave James a pretext to double the size of his army. In future, he could feel more secure against rebellion or invasion.

Unfortunately for James, events in 1685 showed not only the bankruptcy of Whiggery but the limits to the Tories' support. While prepared to vote him an adequate revenue, the Commons would do nothing to benefit the Catholics. In November both Houses expressed concern about James's enlarging the army and his commissioning eighty to ninety Catholic officers, in defiance of the Test Acts. Standing armies were always seen as instruments of absolutism and James's conduct seemed doubly sinister at a time when Louis XIV was using his army to convert Huguenots to

Catholicism. Incensed by what he saw as its groundless suspicion and insubordination, James prorogued the most exuberantly monarchist parliament of the century. It never met again.

Parliament's conduct forced James to rethink his position. If the Tories would not co-operate in repealing the penal laws and Test Acts, James would have, first, to change his strategy and, second, to resort to more dubious methods. On the first point, he would have to abandon the Tories and seek support elsewhere, among the Whigs and, more particularly, the Dissenters. If an Anglican Parliament refused to grant relief to Catholics, a Dissenting Parliament might grant a general toleration embracing both Catholics and Dissenters. To appeal to the Dissenters required a certain psychological adjustment. Although tolerant of individual Dissenters, James's experience (and that of his father) led him to equate religious dissent with political sedition. As he became disillusioned with the Anglicans, he convinced himself that most Dissenters had been driven to defiance by religious persecution. By the end of 1686 he was ready to stake all on an appeal to the Dissenters and confident that his appeal would succeed.

Appealing to the Dissenters raised several problems. Like Catholics, Dissenters were unable to worship freely and suffered various legal disabilities: their exclusion (in principle) from municipal office could prove a serious blow to James's plans for a Parliament, as the great majority of constituencies were boroughs. Since 1680–1 the Crown had sought to harass the Dissenters and break their political influence, putting power firmly into Tory hands. If there was to be any chance of a Dissenting Parliament, the Tories' stranglehold on power in the localities had to be broken and that of the Dissenters built up: indeed, it had to be built up further than their lowly economic and social status warranted. James's plans could succeed, therefore, only if the Dissenters were freed from their disabilities *before* the laws against Dissent were legally repealed and if their local political influence was artificially enhanced. At the same time, James wished to encourage conversions to Catholicism and to allow the small Catholic minority to add its limited weight to the campaign for repeal. In order to achieve these objectives, James had to extend his prerogative in ways which were dubiously legal, which, given his subjects' preconceptions, were bound to provoke fears of absolutism.

The extensions of royal authority were of two types. The first involved the dispensing and suspending powers. Nobody denied that in some cases the king could dispense individuals from the penalties of the law 'where equity requireth a moderation to be had'. He was expected, however, to use such powers sparingly, inquiring fully into the merits of each case. When Charles II suspended the laws against religious nonconformity in 1672, the Commons told him that this was illegal, but this was never confirmed by statute. James considered it morally wrong that he should be denied the services of his Catholic subjects, so appointed some to offices, dispensing them from the penalties of the Test Acts. In June 1686, in the test case *Godden v. Hales*, the judges ruled that the king possessed a dispensing power and could decide when to use it [*Doc. 6*]. Many of James's subjects were unimpressed by the judges' ruling, partly because James had dismissed those judges who thought differently [64] but more because of what followed.

Although it was possible to dispense individual office-holders from complying with the Test Acts, it was impossible to issue individual dispensations to the thousands of Dissenters and Catholics who wished to worship free from the penalties laid down by law. In April 1687 James's Declaration of Indulgence dispensed the whole nation from complying with the penal laws, pending their repeal by Parliament. He thus moved from selective dispensations to the wholesale, if temporary, suspension of a body of laws. This suspending power was legally far more dubious than the dispensing power: statutes could be abrogated only by Parliament. It was made to appear doubly sinister by the suspicions already aroused by James's religion. If he could suspend the penal laws, might he not try to suspend all laws? If he did, nobody's person or property would be safe [*Doc. 7*].

The second extension of royal authority came in the campaign to pack Parliament. To break the Tories' electoral influence and build up that of the Dissenters, James adapted and extended the methods of 1681–5. Tory municipal officials and JPs were replaced by Dissenters (or Catholics); more borough charters were confiscated and new ones issued. In addition, pressure was brought to bear on electors and possible candidates. In the winter of 1686–7 James interviewed MPs from his first Parliament in a last effort to overcome their opposition to repealing the penal laws and Test Acts. Having dissolved that Parliament in July 1687, he ordered that JPs be tendered three questions, which required them to state their position on repeal. Those who were against it were dismissed and replaced by others whom James hoped would prove more tractable. Given the Tory gentry's dominance in the counties, and the wide franchise, James stood little chance of success in the shire elections, so the main thrust of his electoral campaign was in the boroughs. There the electorate was often very small and the franchise disputable, which gave ample scope for fraud and intimidation. Some corporations were purged several times until James was confident that he had found men to do his bidding. In one, the electorate was allegedly reduced to three, of whom two would elect the third. At Huntingdon it was proposed to enrol soldiers as electors; elsewhere army officers were named as candidates. Such manipulation was backed up by canvassing and propaganda. As James aimed especially to win Dissenters' votes, many of his agents were Dissenters, who had learned their trade working for the Exclusionist Whigs [82] [*Docs. 8, 9*].

Both the extension of the dispensing power and the campaign to pack Parliament were inspired by what were (in James's eyes) the purest of motives and merely extended prerogatives and techniques which had previously attracted little criticism, but the extension of these powers beyond traditional limits, together with the suspicion aroused by his religion, made his conduct appear deeply threatening. If by such means he could secure a House of Commons composed of Dissenters, Parliament would cease to be representative of the dominant elements in English society and would become a mere rubber stamp for royal policies. Moreover, once the Test Acts were repealed and Catholics could enter Parliament, similar methods might produce a Papist Parliament which could pass laws against Protestantism. As with the extension of the dispensing power, James's campaign to pack Parliament might have a limited objective – the repeal of the penal laws and Test Acts – but its wider implications were alarming. Together James's actions seemed to threaten to destroy both the laws and the independence of Parliament, the very foundations of the traditional constitution. Moreover, despite James's claim that he wished to allow Catholics the same freedom as others, it was clear that he was heavily biased in their favour and did all he could to silence and intimidate the Anglican clergy. He set up an ecclesiastical commission to punish clergymen who defied his orders not to preach against Catholicism and forced colleges in both universities – the bastions and seminaries of Anglicanism – to admit Catholics.

As James needed a Dissenting Parliament, the Dissenters' reaction to his approaches was crucial. On one hand, his offer of full toleration and free admission to office was very attractive after a generation of persecution. Most Dissenters took advantage of the Indulgence to worship openly, but, on the other hand, when it came to the repeal of the Test Acts, many had grave reservations; besides, the Test Acts affected them far less than the Catholics. They were subjected to conflicting pressures. The king's agents argued that they could make sure of the liberty they now enjoyed only if they repealed the Test Acts as well as the penal laws. They claimed that Dissenters had nothing to fear from the Catholics and that they should be happy to repeal the Test Acts, as a gesture of gratitude.

James's opponents argued that the ultimate aim of the indulgence was to divide Protestants and facilitate the imposition of Catholicism. The bishops, for so long advocates of persecution, now appealed for Protestant unity and held out the prospect of a more broadly based national Church. Perhaps most telling was the pamphlet *A Letter written by Mijn Heer Fagel*, disseminated in large numbers early in 1688. As long as Mary was James's heir presumptive, her attitude to repeal (and William's) was crucial. James tried to persuade them to support it publicly, but while they were ready to agree to toleration, even for Catholics, they refused to endorse the repeal of the Test Acts [*Doc. 11*]. This was stated authoritatively in *Fagel's Letter*, undermining the attempts of James's propagandists to persuade Dissenters that toleration would end when James died. The Letter showed that the Dissenters did not need to pay James's price – the repeal of the Test Acts – for their future liberty [*Doc. 10*].

By the summer of 1688 James had alienated the Anglicans without winning over the Dissenters. Seven bishops petitioned against an order that their clergy should read the Declaration of Indulgence in their churches, which would imply that the Church endorsed it. The petition was printed and the bishops were charged with seditious libel [27]. They were visited in gaol by leading Dissenters, and their acquittal was greeted with a wave of rejoicing which the government could neither prevent nor punish. Meanwhile, there was every sign that the campaign to pack Parliament was failing. James delayed holding a general election and eventually called one only as a panic measure, in the face of imminent invasion; he recalled the writs when it became clear that the gesture had done nothing to regain his subjects' support [95]. But if James's policies were failing and his regime was widely unpopular, it was not on the verge of collapse. Inertia and habits of obedience to authority made rebellion unlikely; the Bloody Assizes had served as a reminder of what happened to unsuccessful rebels. The king had an army of 20,000 which, although mainly Protestant, seemed loyal. The English nobility had long since ceased to keep private armies, and the gentry showed little inclination for war. Scotland was quiet, Ireland's government and army were increasingly controlled by Catholics. James's regime could be challenged only by a professional army from outside the British Isles.

INVASION

William III's position in the Dutch Republic was a peculiar one. The Republic was a federation of seven provinces, of which Holland was much the richest and most influential. Its constitution placed great emphasis on the rights and autonomy of individual provinces and, within each province, those of the major towns. Such a decentralised system was ill-suited to providing decisive leadership, in diplomacy or war. For that, the Republic traditionally looked to its greatest family, the House of Orange. The princes of Orange held various important offices but their power also stemmed from their prestige, as a quasi-royal family, and the individual princes' ability to exploit the complexities of the Republic's political system. There was a continual tension between the provinces' tradition of local autonomy and the princes' efforts to establish a centralised regime, partly for its own sake, partly to enable them to make war more effectively. The provinces and towns accused the princes (especially William III) of seeking to become absolute monarchs; the princes accused their opponents of parochialism, selfishness and corruption.

In 1685, William's foreign policy was hamstrung by the opposition of Amsterdam and the other great towns of Holland. He was convinced that Louis XIV wished to conquer the whole of the Low Countries as the first stage of a plan to dominate Western Europe and to eradicate Protestantism. His opponents believed that William exaggerated the threat from France to provide a pretext to raise an army, which could make him absolute at home. For much of the 1680s they denied him the money and the army he needed for an effective foreign policy. To explain the Revolution of 1688, therefore, one must examine the dramatic change in Dutch public opinion between 1685 and 1688.

William's understanding of James's conduct was even more distorted than that of the English. He greatly overestimated the strength of English republicanism: James had repeatedly told him that the movement for exclusion was a plot against the monarchy. Moreover, most of the English and Scots in the Republic were political or religious exiles, including some republicans. Much of William's information about English affairs came from such people (notably Gilbert Burnet). He accepted stories which were exaggerated or untrue and overestimated the extent and extremism of the opposition to James's policies within England [*Doc. 12*]. He feared that James might provoke a civil war which, if it led (like the last) to a republic, would frustrate his wife's claim to the throne and ruin his chances of bringing England into the next war against France, which he saw as inevitable.

It was not only the danger of civil war which seemed to jeopardise Mary's right to succeed her father. There were rumours that James might alter the succession in favour of a Catholic – perhaps his illegitimate son, the Duke of Berwick. James denied any such intention [*Doc. 3*] but William's anxieties remained. Late in 1687 came a more serious threat: it was announced that James's queen was pregnant. Catholic courtiers expressed confidence that she would produce a son, who would take precedence over Mary in the succession. Suspicious Protestants, who believed the Papists would stick at nothing, expressed doubts as to whether she really was pregnant and remarked cynically that, whether she was or not, the Jesuits would arrange for a boy to appear.

This expectation that a spurious child would be passed off as the queen's underlay William's decision in late April 1688, to invade England 'if he was invited by some men of the best interest to . . . come and rescue the nation and the religion' [*3 vol. III p. 241*]. The invitation, dated 30 June, was signed by only seven men, mostly not of the first rank politically, but it provided a formal justification for a decision that William had already taken. The signatories assured William that the vast majority of people wanted a change and that James's army would not fight [20]. The birth of James's son on 10 June merely confirmed William's decision. Protestants seized on every supposedly suspicious circumstance to support the claim that a monstrous fraud had been perpetrated and that a baby had been smuggled into the queen's bedchamber in a warming-pan. Behind such stories lay a fervent wish that James should have no Catholic heir and they were given credence by the fatuous overconfidence of some Catholics. 'Nothing is more evident' wrote one of William's correspondents 'than that a trick was designed, otherwise they would not have acted like mad people in making the thing disputable, but if they really put the thing in execution or not, God knows. . . . Be it a true child or not, the people will never believe it' [136].

Whatever the English believed, however, events were determined by what happened on the continent. Since 1685 more and more

Dutch people had come to share William's obsessive fear of French attack. The revocation of the Edict of Nantes, the maltreatment of Dutch merchants in France and the influx of Huguenot refugees all helped to revive a dormant sense of Protestant solidarity. Prohibitive new French tariffs damaged Dutch trade to a point where, in commercial terms, the Dutch had nothing to lose from war; this was confirmed when, in September 1688, Louis seized the Dutch wine fleet. Meanwhile Dutchmen were anxious about James's domestic policies and his apparent friendship with France. If he became absolute at home, he would be better able to join the French in attacking the Dutch (as Charles had done in 1672). James was not, in fact, allied to France, but his tactless and inconsistent policy towards William and the Dutch led many to believe that he was and that, sooner or later, James and Louis would attack the Republic. A pre-emptive strike (to prevent England from joining with France) seemed desirable, but it would be dangerous to denude the Republic of troops when Louis might attack at any time. This danger was removed when Louis, fearful of the revival of Habsburg power in Germany, sought to strengthen his eastern frontier by seizing Philippsburg. The attack escalated into a major war, tying down Louis's armies well away from the Dutch frontier and leaving William free to prepare to invade England.

William and the Dutch took great risks in deciding to invade. Not for some months were they sure that the French would be occupied elsewhere. The invasion fleet – much larger than the Spanish Armada of 1588 – required the mobilisation of vast amounts of money and material. William's army of 21,000 was somewhat smaller than James's but much more experienced. James's army was scattered around the country and many regiments were newly raised and incomplete. William preferred not to rely on the assurances of his English friends that James's army would not fight and sought clear military superiority. Even so, all campaigns carried an element of risk – especially in winter – and there was a danger that William could become bogged down in an inconclusive struggle, leaving the Republic exposed to French attack; the States General hired mercenaries from Germany and Sweden to guard against this. His biggest problem, however, lay in getting his army to England. Conventional wisdom stated that it was foolhardy to begin a major naval expedition against the prevailing wind at the onset of winter: when William's fleet first set sail, it was driven back by a storm [78 Ch. 3].

To justify such risks, the rewards of success would have to be very great. If, as seems likely, he aimed from the outset to seize the

Crown, he could not admit it: he had to consider Dutch and English public opinion and his Catholic allies, Spain and the Emperor. Being a pragmatist, he would probably have been satisfied with less. His declaration to the English, printed in French, Dutch and German as well as English, recounted the misdeeds of James's government, demanded an inquiry into the birth of his son and referred all matters to a free Parliament [*Doc. 13*]. (William had been reluctant to put himself at the mercy of parliament, but his English allies had insisted that without this he would win no support.) It seems that his minimum aims were to secure Mary's claim to the succession (by having James's son declared 'suppositious') and to secure a free Parliament which, he assumed, would force James to declare war on France. With England in the war and the succession secure, William could wait for James to die, whereupon he would gain full control of England's resources in his great struggle against France.

William's good fortune was never more apparent than when the wind veered to the east, driving his fleet down the Channel and bottling James's up in the Thames estuary. Devout Protestants saw in this evidence of divine favour, a belief strengthened by William's landing at Torbay on 5 November. Having landed, time was on his side; disillusionment with James and a flood of anti-Catholic propaganda both worked in William's favour. When James became aware of the danger of invasion, he had thrown over the Dissenters and appealed again to his 'old friends', the Tories, but they showed little eagerness to defend him. They were piqued at losing their offices and at his maltreatment of the Church and took at face value William's declaration that he came to secure a free parliament, which they saw as the best cure for the nation's ills. Having been restored to their local offices, the Tories expected to do well in a general election and then to shape a settlement which would prevent James from abusing his power in future, disinherit his son and make the world safe for Tories. Tory militia officers found pretexts not to oppose William's forces, while bishops and Tory peers urged James to call an election and so remove any pretext for William's army to remain in England [47 Ch. 1].

James refused to put himself at his subjects' mercy. He argued that there could be no free election with a foreign army in England. He preferred to rely on his army, even though he had to leave several regiments to keep order in London, where simmering resentment at the opening of Catholic chapels had erupted into violence. It was, however, far from easy to find and engage William's army and there were worrying signs of disaffection in the ranks, especially since James had brought over several Irish Catholic regiments. As James marched westwards, several units deserted, together with certain officers (notably James's nephew, Lord Cornbury, and his protégé, Lord Churchill) from whom he had especial reason to expect total loyalty [38]. Convinced by these defections that he could not rely on his army, and perturbed by the news that in the north many nobles and gentlemen had appeared in arms and that his younger daughter Anne had joined them [77], James's nerve broke. With no prospect of help from France and only too aware that his subjects hated him, he retreated to London and began to negotiate. The conditions which William offered were not unduly harsh. They envisaged James's remaining king, with reduced powers, which would suggest that William was not determined to seize the throne [*Doc. 14*]. James, however, had negotiated only in order to buy time. He was determined to accept no terms, however reasonable. Having sent his wife and son off to France, he slipped away from Whitehall on the night of 10 December and headed for the Kent coast.

James decided to flee partly because he feared for his safety but also because, if a 'free parliament' met, he would have to agree to an inquiry into his son's birth: ' 'Tis my son they aim at and 'tis my son I must endeavour to preserve, whatever becomes of me' [133 *p. 220*]. By fleeing he hoped to avoid unpalatable concessions, but he was seized by a group of fishermen and brought back to London. His flight disconcerted the Tories, who thought it cowardly and irresponsible. He had made no provision for government to continue and had seemed to go out of his way to cause confusion. He destroyed the writs drawn up for a general election and threw the Great Seal in the Thames. Worst of all, he ordered his generals to disband their men without any provision for disarming them first. This could have caused chaos, if most of the officers had not maintained discipline among their men and submitted to William. Even so, London saw two days of serious anti-Catholic rioting, while the provinces were convulsed with rumours that the Irish were coming to murder and pillage.

William's reaction to James's flight was one of quiet satisfaction. James had left of his own volition: nobody could accuse William of driving him out. He might have taken the advice of some of his followers and declared himself king, but for James's return to London. William was clearly annoyed. He had put steady, but unobtrusive pressure on the demoralised king, moving his forces slowly but inexorably towards London; now the pressure would have to be more blatant. In the middle of the night Dutch troops replaced the English guards at Whitehall. James was woken up and advised to leave London 'for his own safety'. On 18 December he left for Rochester, with a guard of Dutch soldiers. This enabled Tories later to forget the ignominy of his first flight and to argue that William had driven him out by force. James's Tory friends begged him not to go, but he was bent on flight and William had no wish to hinder him. He slipped out of a back door which had been left unguarded and landed in France on Christmas morning. Meanwhile, separate assemblies of peers and former members of the Commons invited William to take over the conduct of government, for the time being, and to order a general election for a 'Convention', to meet on 22 January 1689. At last the 'free parliament' which William had demanded was to meet, but without the king who should have summoned it.

PART TWO: THE REVOLUTION SETTLEMENT

2 THE CHANGE OF RULER

By the start of 1689 William was performing many of the functions of a king. He commanded the armed forces (both James's and his own) and directed the civil government. Logic and common sense suggested that his position should be regularised by his being made king. His mother had been a Stuart and he was married to James's daughter, who, if one ignored the Prince of Wales, was his heir. Being recognised as king, however, raised complex problems of political principle and calculation. The divisions between Whig and Tory, so deep in the early 1680s, had been obscured by their common alarm at James's conduct, but revived in the last weeks of 1688. Leading Tories at court pressed James to call a free Parliament, which they hoped would declare the Prince of Wales spurious and pass legislation to prevent future abuses of royal power and secure the interests of the Church against Popery and Dissent – in other words, a return to the Tory dominance of 1685. Judging that William's army offered the best means of bringing James to comply, Tories did little if anything to oppose William and many appeared in arms.

The Whigs, meanwhile, looked to William to rescue them from the political wilderness. Some exiles, who came over with William, urged him to delay calling Parliament until the Whigs could re-establish themselves in local government. Whereas William's declaration referred only to grievances from James's reign, and so had appealed to both Tories and Whigs, Whig activists called for the punishment of those responsible for the Tory reaction of 1681–5. They alleged that there was a continuity of policy between Charles's last years and James's reign and depicted the Tories as the lap-dogs of Stuart absolutism. They claimed that only the Whigs were truly loyal to William's cause and demanded that all those in arms subscribe the Association, a promise to serve William with their lives and fortunes. Many Tories saw this as inconsistent with the oath of allegiance which they had sworn to James, which enabled Whigs to argue that the Tories preferred James to William. In fact, James had treated the Tories and the Church badly and much of the most vociferous criticism of his rule had come from the Anglican clergy [47; 59; 77]. Whatever their reservations about appearing in arms, many – probably most – Tories initially saw William's invasion as a deliverance. 'How these risings and associations can be justified I see not,' wrote Sir John Bramston, 'but yet it is very apparent had not the Prince come, and these persons thus appeared, our religion had been rooted out' [130 *p. 338*].

James's flight forced the Tories into an agonised reappraisal. They now saw that by failing to oppose William they had made possible James's expulsion. Their hopes of regaining power and bringing James to heel evaporated. William seemed more friendly to Whigs and Dissenters than to Tories and Anglicans. Some Tories may have felt guilty at having helped drive James out, however unintentionally, but their guilt was soon subsumed in anger at William's having duped them. On 1 January Sir Edward Seymour told Clarendon that

> all honest men were startled at the manner of the king's being sent from Whitehall; that all the West went in to the Prince of Orange on his declaration, thinking in a free parliament to redress all that was amiss; but that men now began to think that the Prince aimed at something else; and that the countenance he gave the Dissenters gave too much cause of jealousy to the Church of England, who, he said, were the most considerable and substantial body of the nation [5 vol. II *p. 238*]

The rapidly changing political circumstances of the last weeks of 1688 helped to shape the debates about the Crown early in 1689. The Whigs' position was consistent. They argued, both in the Exclusion Crisis and in 1689, that monarchy was a human institution which existed for the benefit of its subjects. Its function was to dispense justice and protect the subject's person and property. This implied that if a monarch misused his powers he should have his powers restricted or, in the last resort, he should be removed. In the Exclusion Crisis, the Whigs argued that James's Catholicism made it virtually certain that he would abuse his powers if he became king. It was thus a matter of self-preservation to exclude him from the succession. The logic of the Whig approach was weakened by their unwillingness to develop the full implications of their ideas. If government existed for the people's good, it presumably originated in some form of popular agreement, which implied in turn that the people could change the government or tell their governors how to rule – and that they could resist their governors if they were dissatisfied with the way they were ruling. Many, though not all, Whigs were reluctant to confront these implications. They were inhibited partly by innate conservatism, but more by the traumatic effect of the events of 1640–60 on the ruling elite. The Exclusionist leaders tried to create an impression of popular insistence on exclusion while confining their agitation to peaceful and lawful channels. They argued that Charles should act on the Commons' advice, but were vague about what would happen if he did not. They talked of Edward II and Richard II, who came to sticky ends after ignoring their subjects' wishes. This implied that subjects had a right to resist their king, but they were wary of saying so explicitly. Only in 1682 did a small minority seriously plan direct action against the king [21].

In 1688 William succeeded where three parliaments had failed: James was excluded without his subjects seriously sullying their hands with rebellion; most of the risings of November and December were ostensibly to protect Protestants against violence from the Catholics [84]. The Whigs were willing, indeed eager, to accept William as king. With their functional, utilitarian view of monarchy they had no qualms about altering the strict line of succession: some more radical Whigs thought it would be easier to curb the power of a king with a weak title. Whigs of all shades of opinion urged that William should be made king – and hoped, in return, for a monopoly of office.

In opposing exclusion, the Tories had laid greater stress than before on the sanctity of the hereditary principle and on the subject's duty not to resist his king. When James fled, they realised that, despite their commitment to non-resistance, they had aided and abetted the expulsion, by force, of the rightful king. Most opposed making William king, partly because it would violate the hereditary succession, partly because they felt that William had tricked them into betraying their principles.

Given the differing views of the two parties, much depended on the outcome of the elections to the Convention. William ostentatiously withdrew the military from the parliamentary boroughs. In some there was confusion as to which charter was in force, but in general the elections were peaceful. Although the party allegiances of the new MPs were not always apparent, it seems clear that a majority of the new House of Commons were Whigs [73].

The Lords had a Tory majority, strengthened by the bishops, which William could do nothing to alter – until he was king, he could not create new peers. Thus agreement could be reached only if the Houses were willing to compromise or if one of them bowed to outside pressure.

There were five possible ways of settling the succession. The first, to invite James back, was soon ruled out. Tories as well as Whigs had found his government intolerable and his decision to desert his kingdom rather than negotiate suggested that he would be most unlikely to agree to any reasonable conditions. Indeed, the Tories conceded the case for his exclusion by agreeing to a motion that experience showed that it was inconsistent with the safety of a Protestant kingdom to be governed by a Popish prince [76]; this would also exclude James's son, whom nobody mentioned, perhaps because, if the Convention investigated the circumstances of his birth, he might turn out not to be spurious after all [99]. A second possibility was for William to be sole monarch. William liked this idea, but his English supporters did not. Admiral Herbert, who commanded the invasion fleet, said that he would not have done so had he known William could behave so badly towards his wife, while the Tories would never agree to an arrangement which made William's conquest of England so obvious. Most Tories wished to preserve James's theoretical right to the Crown and to avoid tampering with the succession, so proposed making William and Mary regents for James. They argued that James had forfeited only his right to exercise the powers of the Crown, not his title. Against this, the Whigs (and a few Tories) claimed that it was impractical to separate the exercise of royal power from the title and that if James was not deprived of his title he might return. The regency proposal was heavily defeated in the Commons and rejected by three votes in the Lords.

This left two possibilities. After the failure of the regency proposal, the Tory majority in the Lords claimed that, with James's departure, the Crown had already passed to Mary as next heir. This would prevent James's return and do as much as possible to maintain the hereditary principle. It would remove any need for Parliament to meddle with the succession: some had grave doubts about the Convention's legal status and doubted whether it had the power to choose who should be monarch. It would also salve the consciences of the Tories who had argued that the hereditary principle was sacrosanct.

The Commons refused to adopt this solution. A majority of MPs favoured the fifth possible solution – offering the Crown jointly to William and Mary. Such a dual monarchy would be exceptional and could not easily be reconciled with the theory of a hereditary succession. So abnormal an arrangement could not be made by any authority other than Parliament. Some MPs wanted the offer of the Crown to come explicitly from Parliament, because they wished to attach conditions to the offer. 'Before the question be put, who shall be set upon the throne,' said Lord Falkland, 'I would consider what powers we ought to give the crown, to satisfy them that sent us hither' [7 vol. ix *p. 30*]. Making William and Mary king and queen would also give some recognition of the risks which William had run and the expense he had incurred, as well as satisfying MPs' prejudices concerning the proper relationship of husband and wife. In the words of Henry Pollexfen, if Mary 'be now proclaimed queen, can anything be more desirable than that her husband be joined with her in the government? . . . Does any think the Prince of Orange will come in to be a subject to his own wife in England? This is not possible, nor ought to be in nature' [7 vol. ix *p. 64*].

Thus the Lords argued that Mary was already queen, the Commons that the Convention should offer the Crown jointly to William and Mary. The two Houses sought to resolve their differences in a conference on 6 February. Ostensibly, the conference was concerned, not with the succession but with what had happened to James. The Commons had resolved on 28 January

> that King James II, having endeavoured to subvert the constitution of the kingdom, by breaking the original contract between king and people; and by the advice of Jesuits and other wicked persons having violated the fundamental laws; and having withdrawn himself out of this kingdom; has abdicated the government; and that the throne is thereby vacant. [84 *p. 48*]

The Lords objected to the word 'abdicated', preferring the more neutral term 'deserted', and also to the suggestion that the throne was vacant, which implied that the Convention had the right to fill it [*Doc. 18*]. The debate ranged around these points, but the Lords' underlying concern was clearly to prevent William's being made king [94].

It was William who resolved the deadlock. Mindful of both English and international opinion, he was careful to avoid any appearance of military conquest: at each stage he had acted, apparently, at the behest of the English. He had demanded an invitation to invade, he had come to London only when invited by the City authorities, he had taken on the government only when invited and he had hoped for an unsolicited invitation to become king. Nevertheless, it was his military power that had driven James out and his invasion army remained, conspicuously, close to London. The Lords' obstruction annoyed him. A quick settlement was essential. Some of James's old regiments were mutinous and the Protestant minority in Ireland was being overrun by the Catholics. The longer a settlement was delayed, the greater were the fears that radicals and republicans might profit from the confusion. William, therefore, summoned some leading peers and told them that he would not act as regent, nor would he be subordinate to his wife. As a mere consort he would lack a clearly defined position and his authority would lapse if his wife died before him (as Philip II's had on the death of Mary Tudor). Thus if the Lords would not agree with the Commons to make him king on his own terms, he would go home and leave the English to cope with the ensuing confusion. To sweeten the pill, he agreed that Mary's sister Anne and her children should succeed before any children he might have by a later marriage [*Doc. 15*].

Faced with William's firm stand, the Lords' resolution crumbled. Some Tory peers slipped away and the House resolved to concur with the Commons and that the Crown should be offered to William and Mary. The next week was spent in waiting for Mary to come from Holland and in completing the list of 'conditions' upon which the Crown should be offered (which became the Declaration of Rights). On 13 February the Crown was offered formally to William and Mary, who were first read the Declaration, now expanded to include the arrangements for the succession which William had proposed and a new oath of allegiance. The Crown was to pass as if James were dead (ignoring his son), first to Mary and her heirs, then to Anne and her heirs and finally to any heirs whom William might have by a later marriage. Thus the Convention tried to maintain the hereditary principle as far as was possible. James was declared to have abdicated and William was joined with his wife in an unprecedented dual monarchy, although he alone was to direct the government. However, when it came to the *transmission* of the right to the throne, the Convention had adhered to the hereditary principle, the right being passed on first by Mary, then by Anne, and finally by William.

3 THE SIGNIFICANCE OF THE CHANGE OF RULER

Later generations regarded the change of ruler in 1689 as very significant, but interpreted what happened in those few days in the Convention with the benefit of hindsight or in the light of the politics of their own day. Much subsequent misunderstanding stemmed from the publication, barely a year after the event, of Locke's *Two Treatises of Government* [14]. Locke's avowed purpose was to justify the Revolution and his *Second Treatise* seemed, in retrospect, to provide a logical and lucid analysis of what had happened.

Locke claimed that men were rational beings, who formed themselves into political societies for their individual and collective good. Such societies made possible the creation of a framework of laws to resolve disputes, which in a state of nature could be settled only by force. Political societies were formed by a voluntary 'original compact', whereby men agreed to abandon some of the rights and liberty they had previously enjoyed and to submit to a common set of laws. This original consent was renewed, tacitly, as each new generation grew up to enjoy the protection of the laws. The laws were amended, or extended, by a legislature entrusted with that task by the people. They were enforced by an executive, which should ideally be part of the legislature but should not dominate it, since the combination of legislative and executive powers in the hands of one man, or a few, was likely to lead to tyranny. If such tyranny arose, the government was dissolved. The people were absolved from their duty to obey it and could set up another in its place [*Doc. 17*].

In considering the usefulness of the *Two Treatises* in understanding the Revolution, one should ask, first, whether they marked a new departure in English political and constitutional thought and, second, how far Locke's account of the dissolution and reconstitution of government fitted the facts of 1689. On the first point, Locke had much in common with some of the more radical thinkers of the 1640s, notably the Levellers, whose very radicalism, and identification with civil war and regicide, led to the marginalisation or rejection of their arguments after 1660. The bulk of political discourse in Restoration England continued to be couched in terms of law and history. The 'ancient constitution' was seen as an organic growth, dating back beyond the days of written records and enshrining the wisdom of untold generations. Nobody could tell when the laws, or the powers of the king, or the rights of the subject had originated, but they were seen as having grown in a symbiotic relationship and could best be defined by means of precedents.

Such a historical approach could pose problems. Precedents were of little help in dealing with unprecedented circumstances, like those of 1641–2. They could also prove embarrassing. Historical research showed that William I had arbitrarily imposed new laws on England after the Conquest: might not later kings, equally arbitrarily, revoke those laws or impose new ones? Some claimed that it was illogical to suggest that laws could evolve independently. Some authority – presumably a king – must have enacted and enforced those laws, which implied that absolute monarchy was more natural than limited monarchy. Despite such problems, the will to believe in the ancient constitution was immensely strong.

Locke did not invent the idea that monarchy should be limited or that kings should rule in the interests of their people. Such beliefs were central to the theory and practice of the ancient constitution: English kings were unable to impose taxes or make laws without the consent of Parliament. Locke parted company from the mainstream of English constitutional thought by abandoning the argument from English history. He used illustrations from antiquity or the Old Testament, but his system drew its force, not from historical examples, but from a theoretical argument about the origins and ends of government. In this, he had much in common with Hobbes (hardly a 'mainstream' figure). Both agreed that governments were artificial constructs – no one form was inherently superior to another, or had the stamp of divine approval. Both saw government in utilitarian terms: it had to serve a practical purpose, not enforce any particular set of values. But whereas Hobbes saw men as violent and irrational, Locke saw them as rational and wise. Whereas Hobbes saw the task of government as protecting men from violence, Locke saw it as protecting property and the right to a peaceful and prosperous existence. Whereas Hobbes argued that government needed despotic power to perform its functions, Locke argued that its power should be limited. Finally, whereas Hobbes argued that submission to government should be absolute and unconditional so long as its protection continued, for Locke submission was always conditional on the government's fulfilling its responsibilities, which extended well beyond mere physical protection.

Although Locke differed from most Whigs in abandoning the argument from history, the thrust of his argument was similar to that of the Exclusionists; indeed, he wrote most of the *Two Treatises* during the Exclusion Crisis [21]. Locke, however, developed to the full those implications of the Exclusionists' arguments which they had been reluctant to draw. They had talked mainly of the king's moral obligation to govern in his people's best interests and to follow the Commons' advice. Talk of such an obligation might imply that there was some sort of contract between ruler and ruled, but there is almost no mention of 'contract' or 'compact' in the surviving parliamentary debates of Charles II's reign. The concept of contract was familiar enough in law, but seems rarely to have been used in constitutional discussions before 1689. It should be made clear that Locke did not talk of a contract between ruler and ruled. His 'original compact' occurred when a political society was formed. When the members of that society established a government they did so, not by a 'contract', but in the form of a 'trust'. A contract gave the ruler rights and obligations. A trust imposed upon him only obligations. He was given power to serve particular ends. If he failed to achieve those ends, the trust could be terminated [*Doc. 17*].

With the concept of a trust, Locke gave theoretical form to the old belief that a ruler should rule in his subjects' interests. That view had often been expressed using the analogy of 'patriarchal' authority: a father would, by the law of nature, do what was best for his children. This analogy implied that a king's authority over his people was like a father's over his family – inherent in his position and thus unquestionable, part of the natural order of things. Locke was inspired to write the *Two Treatises* by the publication of Sir Robert Filmer's extreme restatement of the patriarchal view. Locke denied that anybody exercised authority as of right: it had to be vested in them by the political community, which implied that it could be taken away if it was not used for the purpose for which it had been given. The criteria for taking back this authority were not objective (the breach of certain fixed rules) but subjective – the people believed that the ruler was not ruling as he should. It was up to the people as a whole to decide when their ruler ceased to act for their good and degenerated into a tyrant. When that happened all obligations of obedience were dissolved and the people could resist him – by force if necessary – remove him and establish what government they chose in his place [*Doc. 17*].

In this Locke moved well beyond the norms of Whig thought. Whigs might agree that people were justified in defending their homes against robbers or against Catholic soldiers, enlisted contrary to law, but memories of civil war and the natural conservatism of property owners made most Whigs reluctant to endorse the right of resistance in any but the most restricted cases. They certainly were not prepared to grant it to the people in general, as Locke did, or to allow the people to set up what form of government they chose. If that were permitted, what would happen to the ancient constitution – or the hegemony of the landed elite? Locke argued that experience suggested that people would move against the government only under extreme provocation and that, if the government were re-established, it would probably be very much along traditional lines. Even so, his theory smacked unpleasantly of anarchy to many moderate Whigs. Whereas for Locke sovereignty lay in the people, for most Whigs it lay in parliament, in the ancient trinity of king, Lords and Commons. This concept had tradition behind it, but begged the question of what to do if one of the three elements was missing, as in 1689, or if the three could not agree among themselves, as in 1642 or in 1679–81.

Locke, then, took familiar, often semi-developed concepts and expressed them in an abstract theoretical form at variance with the concrete, historical ways of thinking of the ancient constitution. He also developed his arguments far beyond the point which most Whigs regarded as safe or desirable. They wished to be freed from the dangers of 'Popery and arbitrary government', not to give ordinary people the power to overthrow established authority or to refashion the constitution. As a result, Locke's influence was limited in the generation after 1689. Most Whigs still argued from history or took the Revolution itself as the starting-point of a new constitutional order.

This brings us to the question of how far Locke's *Two Treatises* described what happened in 1688–9. In a sense, one should not expect them to. Locke's insistence on arguing in general terms, his use of subjective criteria of acceptability and his avoidance of arguments from history make the *Treatises* unspecific. It is hard to see anything directly relating to England in the discussion of the origins of government, but the same is not true when he discusses how governments can be dissolved. The hypothetical constitution which he considers closely resembles England's, with a king and bicameral legislature. Several of the ways in which a government can be dissolved could refer directly to James II: for example, through a king setting his will above the laws or tampering with elections. How far, then, can James's removal be seen in Lockean terms?

First, the question of a 'trust'. The Convention's debates contain few references to the monarch's power being a 'trust' from the people, but there are many references to a 'compact' or 'original contract'. The Commons' resolution of 28 January referred to James's 'breaking the original contract between king and people', but most of those who used the phrase were vague as to what it meant. A few saw it as a historical event, the very beginning of government. Others saw it as the exchange of oaths, whereby the king swore at his coronation to rule according to law and the people swore an oath of allegiance. Most, however, used the term so vaguely that one cannot tell what they understood by it. Its appearance in 1689 perhaps represents an attempt to articulate a sense of betrayal, felt by Tories as well as Whigs. They believed that James had failed to fulfil his obligations to his people and felt that this absolved them from their obligations to him. If the term was much used, it does not, however, seem to have been clearly understood. On 29 January the Lords summoned a group of lawyers and asked them what the original contract was. Sir Robert Atkyns is recorded as saying:

> I believe none of us have it in our books or cases; not anything that touches on it. Thinks it must refer to the first original of government. Thinks the king never took any government but there was an agreement between king and people. It is a limited monarchy and a body politic and the king head of it. If there were an original contract yet it is subject to variations as the times. [134 *p. 15*]

Sir Edward Nevill put it more succinctly: 'It must of necessity be implied by the nature of government' [134, *p. 15*] [*Doc. 20*]. It is, therefore, doubtful whether the men of 1689, despite the language they used, had a Lockean view of the original contract, or of a ruler's trust, in any but the most embryonic form. At most, the idea of 'contract' provided a way of expressing the feeling that James had failed to rule as he should [94].

Was he, therefore, deposed for breaking the original contract? A quick reading of the resolution of 28 January might suggest that he was, but the Commons concluded that he had 'abdicated the government'. The resolution as a whole is ambiguous. One could argue that the 'abdication' followed directly from James's 'having withdrawn himself out of the kingdom', with the remaining clauses, about contract and the fundamental laws, being merely illustrative. One could also argue that James's breaches of the law and of the original contract were as much part of his abdication as was his leaving the country: they were all part of the process whereby he showed his unfitness to rule [84].

To explain this ambiguity we must consider the circumstances of the Convention. Locke was one man writing a work of theory. The Convention was a large and politically divided body, unsure of its legal status, struggling with the practical problem of settling the succession before William went home in disgust or the country collapsed into anarchy or republicanism. Many Whigs in the Commons doubtless believed that James had forfeited his right to rule and ought to be deposed: Jack Howe said in 1694: 'I was for deposing King James and setting up King William' [7]. There might just have been enough who felt that way to have secured a majority in the Commons in favour of deposition, but it would never have passed the Lords; they were more likely to accept the argument that 'we do not depose him; it is his own act' [10 vol. II *p. 407*]. For many Whigs the really important thing was to remove James and put William and Mary in his place. As long as that happened, the precise form of James's removal and the finer points of constitutional theory were comparatively unimportant. Some Whigs, indeed, probably doubted whether the Convention had the right to depose a king.

For these reasons the question of deposing James never really arose. The Whigs chose to argue that he had abdicated, thus placing the blame where they believed it belonged. The Tories might have been expected to welcome this argument, as a way of getting rid of James without deposing him. In fact, they showed distinct reservations about it. Even after the rejection of a regency, some still argued that James had forfeited only the exercise of kingly power, not his right to be king. Some complained that the term 'abdication' was unknown to English law. (The Whigs replied that the same was true of 'desertion', the term the Tories preferred.) Some who saw the abdication solely in terms of James's withdrawal claimed that he had been driven out by William's troops. Above all, the Tories resented the linking of the abdication with the alleged vacancy of the throne. If the throne was vacant, it implied that Parliament could fill it, but since the Exclusion Crisis the Tories had asserted vehemently that Parliament could not determine the succession. Moreover, only if Parliament could fill the throne could it offer it jointly to William and Mary, and the Tories were determined to keep William out if they could. They, therefore, claimed that the throne was not vacant, although the Lords coyly refused to say who actually occupied it.

However, if (as they claimed) the Crown could pass only by the normal method of descent, it could pass only to Mary. The Tories, therefore, insisted that for Parliament to fill the throne would make the monarchy elective, a claim which the Whigs vehemently denied.

The arguments about the finer shades of meaning of 'abdication' and 'desertion' are far removed from the Lockean view of a people deposing their ruler for betraying his trust. Two other Lockean concepts must also be considered: the right of resistance and the dissolution of government. When William came over with an army and various aristocrats rose against James, it might seem obvious that they were engaged in resistance, but few admitted this. Those who assembled at Nottingham on 22 November 1688 declared: 'We own it rebellion to resist a king that governs by law, but he was always accounted a tyrant that made his will his law; and to resist such an one we justly esteem no rebellion, but a necessary defence' [84 *pp.* 46–7] – sentiments which Locke certainly shared. Lord Wharton told the Commons that he had helped to drive James out and would willingly do so again. In general, however, such arguments seemed both unnecessary (since the main emphasis was on James's abdication, not his deposition) and dangerous: with the country, it seemed, teetering on the brink of anarchy, it must have seemed most unwise to assert the people's right to resist their rulers.

For much the same reasons there was little talk of the dissolution of government. Lady Mordaunt wrote to Locke that here was 'an occasion not only of mending the government but of melting it down and making all new' [14 *p. 58*]. Interestingly, Locke did not agree. He wrote on 29 January: 'The settlement of the nation upon the sure grounds of peace and security is put into their [the Convention's] hands, which can no way so well be done as by restoring our ancient government, the best possibly that ever was, if taken and put together all of a piece in its original constitution' [135 vol. III *p. 545*]. Lord Wharton, while prepared to justify having resisted James, said that, when it came to settling the government, 'I hope it will be done as near the ancient government as can be' [7 vol. IX *p. 29*]. Although one or two anxious Tories argued that the government had not been dissolved, hardly any of the Whigs suggested that it had. James's abdication, they argued, left a void at the top of the structure of government, but otherwise it remained essentially unchanged. 'The constitution, notwithstanding the vacancy, is the same,' said Sir John Maynard, 'the laws that are the foundations and rules of that constitution are the same' [16 vol. V *p. 72*]. The void, or vacancy, had been created by James, not by the people. The task of the people, or rather its representatives, was to fill it. This was a matter not of ideology, but of pragmatism. James had left them without a government, so they had the choice between perpetual anarchy or providing for themselves [*Doc. 19*].

For these reasons it is misleading to see the Revolution as a triumph for Whig ideology – if one interprets 'Whig ideology' in a Lockean sense. If anybody showed a stubborn attachment to ideology in 1689 it was the Tories. They argued inflexibly that for Parliament to determine the succession would make the Crown elective [*Doc. 18*]. Beneath this inflexibility lay not only an obstinate determination to prevent William from becoming king, but also a real commitment to principle. Since the Exclusion Crisis, the Tories had developed a powerful and coherent ideology based on the exaltation of royal power, the hereditary principle and non-resistance. It was an authoritarian ideology, well suited to a party with aristocratic leaders and a hierarchically organised Church, in which authority flowed down from the top. It seemed especially appropriate at a time of renewed fears of civil war and social upheaval. Whereas there was some tension between the Whigs' social conservatism and their sporadic demagogy, the Tories' political and social outlooks blended naturally together. The great flaw in Tory ideology was the assumption that the king would respect the law, protect the Church and rely on Tory support. As long as he did so, the Tories' exaltation of royal authority made sound political sense. James's unexpected behaviour left the Tories confused and bitter. A minority, like Danby, opposed him openly. Most found themselves left behind by events, with little choice but to acquiesce in a change of ruler which they had not wanted. A few (mostly clergy) refused to swear allegiance to William and Mary and lost their places. Most salved their consciences by recognizing the new rulers as *de facto* and not *de jure* monarchs (rulers in fact, but not by right), which was made easier by the omission of 'rightful and lawful' from the new oath of allegiance [*Doc. 42*].

While most Tories sooner or later swallowed all the oaths that were tendered to them, there is no doubt that many suffered qualms of conscience. Their emotional attachment to monarchy remained strong. Despite the gloomy prophecies of elective monarchy, there was every reason to expect the break in the hereditary line to be only temporary. Once James and William were dead, the succession would flow back into its proper channel. Such expectations were frustrated by the death of Anne's last surviving child, the Duke of Gloucester, in 1700. Mary had died without children in 1694 and William showed no inclination to remarry, so it was clear that the Protestant Stuart line would end with Anne. This left a choice between James's son, the 'Old Pretender', who was being raised as a Catholic in France, or the nearest Protestant relative, Sophia, Electress of Hanover, who was descended from James I's daughter. In 1689 Anne's prodigious fecundity seemed to offer the certain prospect of a Protestant Stuart dynasty, which meant that the Tories would not, in the long run, have to choose between Protestantism and legitimism. After Gloucester's death they had to face that choice. They plumped for Protestantism, for Hanover, but with an ill-disguised reluctance, expressed in a last doomed wallow in divine-right emotionalism under Anne [55].

The Revolution had not killed the Tories' belief in either divine right or hereditary monarchy, although it dealt a body-blow to the idea that hereditary right was indefeasible: the resolution against Catholic monarchs, which the Tories accepted, introduced a conditional element which they had earlier denied [68, Chapter by Nenner; 76]. If they had not taken the sacred attributes of monarchy so seriously, they would not have made such difficulties about making William king. Their truculence towards him reflected, not an abandonment of their reverence for monarchy, but a gut feeling that William was not a proper monarch. With Anne's accession the Tory veneration for monarchy resurfaced, although this did not prevent Tory politicians from trying, like the Whigs, to force their wishes on the queen. Tory pulpits rang again with the rhetoric of non-resistance. For centuries it had been believed that a monarch's 'royal touch' could cure scrofula; suspended under William, this practice was revived for the last time, by Anne. It was George I's accession, not William's, that killed off belief in divine right. In 1689 the Tories could look forward to the day when Anne would become queen. In 1714, their fatuous hopes that the Pretender might turn Protestant were soon dashed, after which there was no future for the Anglican legitimism which had been the backbone of Toryism. It was not so much the events of 1688–9 as Queen Anne's gynaecological problems which destroyed the Tories' attachment to hereditary monarchy and divine right.

If the change of ruler in 1688–9 marked neither the triumph of Locke's view of the constitution, nor a defeat for Tory ideology, what was its significance in the history of ideas, apart from inspiring Locke to publish the work he had written almost a decade earlier? It marked a victory for a Whig view of the constitution more modest and untheoretical than Locke's. The generation after 1689 saw only a limited development of the theory of contract, which still tended to be equated with the ancient constitution [*Doc. 20*]. Writers continued to claim that England's was a mixed and balanced constitution, with an increasing emphasis on the separation of powers [*Doc. 21*].

The Whigs' approach to the constitution was essentially pragmatic. In 1689 they did not worry overmuch about the origins of political authority. They were ready to adopt the fiction of James's abdication, which enabled them to remove him from the throne without deposing him. When asked what authority they had to name his successor, they appealed to common sense and the right of self-preservation: if they did not fill the throne, chaos would follow. They did not see this as a precedent: a situation so extraordinary could hardly be expected to arise again. They avoided awkward theoretical questions and concentrated on patching up the old constitution and getting it working again. Their arguments rested on vague concepts of expediency and the public good [*Doc. 19*]. These could be found in Locke, but for most Whigs Parliament (not the people as a whole) was to decide what was in the public interest. Such nebulous guiding principles could lead to flexibility, inconsistency, even cynicism. It is hard to think of any principle embraced by part or all of the Whig party in the 1690s which had not been betrayed by at least some of its leaders by 1720. After 1689 the days of the Tories' attachment to ideology were numbered. The future lay with the Whigs and with the politics of pragmatism, expediency and cynicism [85].

4 THE CONSTITUTIONAL SETTLEMENT

On 28 January the Commons resolved that James had abdicated and that the throne was vacant. Next day a committee was appointed to 'bring in general heads of such things as are absolutely necessary to be considered for the better securing our religion, laws and liberties' [131, *p. 15*]. 'Before any person was named to fill the throne', wrote Sir John Reresby, 'they would frame conditions upon which only he should be accepted as king and tie him up more strictly to the observance of them than other princes had been before' [17 *p. 546*]. This reflected bitter experience of the Stuarts. 'Because King Charles II was called home by the Convention and nothing settled, you found the consequence', said Sir William Williams [7 vol. IX *p. 30*]. On 2 February the committee brought in a list of twenty-eight heads. It was a somewhat motley list, many of them reflecting the interests or grievances of individual committee members. The House noted that some re-affirmed existing rights and laws, but others would change the laws and so require legislation; it ordered the committee to separate the two elements. It reported back on the 7 February, with its recommendations divided into two sections [*Doc. 22*]. The first, declaratory section contained twelve heads, all of which had appeared in the first list; a general reference to parliament's privileges now became a specific claim to freedom of speech and of debate. The second listed twenty heads on which legislation was needed. Several points appeared in both sections – for example, the need for free elections and frequent parliaments. Two of the original heads had disappeared – the provisions that no pardon could be pleaded to an impeachment and that parliament should remain in session until all necessary business had been completed [110].

The committee reported on the afternoon of the 7th. That morning the Commons heard that the Lords had concurred with their resolution of 28 January and had voted to offer the Crown to William and Mary. The Lords also sent down a new oath of allegiance, without the phrase 'rightful and lawful'. It was proposed that the Commons should join in this offer of the Crown, but after some debate it was resolved to consider the committee's report first. Most of those who advocated this order of proceeding were Whigs, but it was a Tory, Sir Robert Sawyer, who proposed an addition to the second section (approved by the House) that Catholics be excluded from the throne. The debate resumed next day. A committee now recommended that the first section of the heads (the restatement of existing rights) should be joined to the Lords' votes on the offer of the Crown and the new oath of allegiance, while the second section should be dropped. Despite some opposition, this proposal was adopted. The Commons concurred in the vote to offer the Crown to William and Mary, agreed to the new oath of allegiance and sent these up to the Lords, together with the statement of rights and proposals on the order which the succession should follow after William and Mary. The Lords agreed next day to the provisions for the succession, but disagreed with the wording of some of the heads in the statement of rights. They disliked the unequivocal condemnation of the dispensing power which, if properly used, could be useful to the subject. The Commons agreed to add the rider 'as it hath been assumed and exercised of late' and to omit the last phrase from the provision that parliaments 'ought to be held frequently and suffered to sit'. The Commons were also persuaded to add the phrase 'as allowed by law' to the statement of the right of Protestants to keep arms for their own defence: clearly the peers feared that this might otherwise tend towards 'arming the mob'. The differences between the Houses were settled on the 12th and on the 13th the whole package was read to William and Mary, just before they were offered the Crown.

It is unclear why the Commons decided to drop the second part of the list of rights and grievances. Various explanations have been offered, but two seem plausible. The first was a pragmatic decision to concentrate on the possible. The second section was a declaration of intent, not a binding commitment: some MPs doubted whether the Convention, which had not (like a lawful Parliament) been summoned by a king, had the power to impose conditions on anybody. Some of the proposals later became law, but many did not. Passing new laws would take time and would probably lead to further disputes with the Lords; given the unsettled state of the country, speed was essential.

The other decisive factor was, again, William. His supporters in the Commons urged the House to concentrate on restating known rights. He clearly disliked some elements of even the modified document and considered vetoing it when it was made into a bill. He denied letting it be known, informally, that he was against the novel restrictions in the original document, but many believed that this was his opinion and that those who advocated such restrictions were unlikely to enjoy his favour. It is also worth remarking that, as when he insisted on being made king, he was in a very powerful position. There was still a large Dutch military presence in the environs of London – and there was the danger that, if he were dissatisfied, he might go home and plunge the country into confusion [57; 74; 78].

The Declaration's legal status was uncertain. The concern shown by both Houses and by William about its wording and contents, and the ceremony surrounding its reading to William and Mary, would suggest that it was seen as containing conditions which they had to accept before ascending the throne [110]. However, there was no explicit link between the offer of the Crown and acceptance of the 'rights' in the Declaration. After these had been recited, the Declaration referred to the Houses'

> entire confidence that his said Highness, the Prince of Orange, will perfect a deliverance so far advanced by him; and will still preserve them from the violation of their rights, which they have here asserted; and from all other attempts upon their religion, rights and liberties. [99 *p. 303*]

In his reply, William did not promise to abide by the provisions of the Declaration. He told the Houses 'as I had no other intention in coming hither than to preserve your religion, laws and liberties, so you may be sure that I shall endeavour to support them' [99 *p. 304*]. One could thus see the Declaration as informing the new monarchs how Charles and James had abused their powers, with the implication that they should avoid such abuses; it was not a formal contract [99]. Later in 1689, the Declaration was turned into a bill, which would not have seemed necessary had it been regarded as an unequivocal contract. The first bill was lost by prorogation after a series of disputes between the Houses. The second passed with little difficulty [74; 110].

As eventually passed, the Bill differed from the Declaration in prohibiting dispensations (except where specifically allowed by statute) and barring any Catholic, or spouse of a Catholic, from becoming king or queen of England. Although both Houses had passed resolutions to this effect in January and such a provision had been added to the second section of the heads of grievances, this became law only with the Bill of Rights and remains so to this day. When William gave his assent to the Bill of Rights, he at last bound himself formally to adhere to the terms of the Declaration. But how far did these terms impose novel and effective limitations on the Crown? Most referred to specific abuses of royal prerogatives during the 1680s, but did not call into question the prerogatives themselves. The suspending power was declared illegal and the dispensing power severely restricted, which, given James's stretching of a judgment in favour of the dispensing power, is hardly surprising. Some clauses referred as much to Charles's reign as to James's – for example, the assertion of the right of petitioning or the condemnation of abuses of the legal system. Several declared that parliament should meet frequently and that elections and debates should be free, sentiments which were conventional enough and reflected resentment at recent attempts to intimidate MPs and tamper with elections.

The most striking novelty was the statement 'that the raising or keeping a standing army within the kingdom in time of peace, unless it be with consent of parliament, is against law' [20 *p. 28*]. The army's legal position had long been uncertain. Charles II was the first king to possess a standing army, usually referred to euphemistically as 'guards and garrisons'. It was not large and was widely dispersed, at home and abroad, but when he raised additional land forces for war, in 1673 and 1678, Parliament expressed serious anxieties about the danger of military rule and absolutism. The common law did not regard mutiny and desertion as crimes and would not recognise the courts martial which the Crown set up to punish them. After James's reign, such indeterminacy could no longer be tolerated. The Bill of Rights made it clear that the king could not keep up any permanent land forces without parliament's explicit approval: tacit connivance was no longer sufficient. Moreover, starting in 1689, a series of mutiny acts were passed, allowing the punishment of mutiny and desertion by martial law, but for only a limited period, usually a year. Thus parliament could revoke the right to hold courts martial simply by failing to pass a new act.

By these means parliament asserted its control over military discipline and the army's very existence. However, most of the Bill of Rights' other constitutional provisions restated what most people regarded as the constitution, clarifying grey areas which the Stuarts had exploited. Some were very vague: 'Election of Members of Parliament ought to be free'. How was one to define 'free'? Even if one could define it, the Bill made no provision for ensuring that elections were in fact free, and this was a crucial weakness: it contained no mechanism for its own enforcement. And yet it came to be seen as a major constitutional document, almost on a par with Magna Carta. As early as 1690, one MP called it 'our original contract'. The assertion of the 'right to bear arms' and the prohibition of 'cruel and unusual　punishments' both　became amendments to the United States constitution. In explaining this apparent anomaly, we must look beyond the terms of the Bill itself. If the limitations on the monarchy which it outlined did, in fact, become established, along with many others, this owed little to the generalities of the Bill. The main reason must be sought in the changed relationship of Crown and Parliament, which had its origins not in constitutional changes but in the Revolution financial settlement.

5 THE FINANCIAL SETTLEMENT

From the start some MPs saw the royal finances as the key to any settlement. The Convention of 1660 had assessed the Crown's annual expenditure as £1,200,000 (including the army and navy). Charles was granted a number of revenues, notably the customs, excise and hearth tax, which were expected to yield that amount. In the 1660s the yield fell well short, but in the 1670s and 1680s it improved greatly, thanks to a boom in overseas trade and more efficient collection. Charles had, at first, reverted to the old practice of tax farming. A group of financiers would undertake to collect a tax, paying the king an annual rent and keeping all they collected in excess of that rent. This had the advantage of ensuring prompt and regular revenue payments, while the farmers proved a useful source of loans to a government with constant cash-flow problems and poor credit. Its great disadvantage was that, if trade expanded rapidly, the farmers profited, not the Crown. By 1685 tax farming had been abandoned and the three major revenues were collected by salaried officials. The yield of the ordinary revenue had grown to around £1,500,000 a year, sufficient to enable Charles to survive without Parliament. James II's Parliament granted him the same revenues, without enquiring into their current yield.

At the Restoration, the Commons returned to the principle that the king should 'live of his own', that he should normally subsist on revenues enjoyed in perpetuity or granted for life, but were careful not to give so much that he would have no need of parliaments. The main change was that before the civil wars much Crown revenue had come from land and feudal rights, which the king enjoyed as his own property, or from the misuse of his prerogative. After 1660 all the Crown's major revenues were granted by parliament, but the basic distinction was maintained between ordinary revenue (granted for life or forever, to cover normal expenditure) and extraordinary revenue (voted for a limited period, for wars or other emergencies).

When Charles II complained that his ordinary revenue was

inadequate, the Commons voted him extraordinary supplies rather than increase it. Despite such precautions, however, Charles ended up able to live without Parliament. The men of 1689 were determined not to make the same mistake. On 29 January William Sacheverell told the Commons: 'Secure this House, that parliaments be duly chosen and not kicked out at pleasure which never could have been done without such an extravagant revenue that they might never stand in need of parliaments' [7 vol. IX *p. 33*]. To William Harbord, the financial settlement was the crucial question. 'You have an infallible security for the administration of the government. All the revenue is in your own hands, which fell with the last king, and you may keep that back. Can he whom you place on the throne support the government without the revenue?' [7 vol. IX *p. 36*]. On 26 February Whigs like Birch and Pulteney joined with Tories like Clarges and Seymour to urge that William be granted the revenue for no longer than three years [*Doc. 23*]. It was decided to investigate the revenue's current yield before coming to any decision.

Impatient at the Commons' dilatoriness, William offered to give up the unpopular hearth tax, which had been granted in perpetuity. They accepted his offer, but extended the customs for three months only. In the words of Sir William Williams 'If you give the crown too little you may add at any time, if once you give too much, you will never have it back again' [7 vol. IX *p. 177*]. On 20 March they resolved to settle on the king a revenue of £1,200,000 a year, but this figure was arrived at without investigating the king's needs and was insufficient even in peacetime, let alone on the eve of war: since James had gone to France, it seemed inevitable that England would sooner or later be drawn into the struggle on the continent. The Commons decided that half this figure would suffice for the civil administration (a gross underestimate), so that the other £600,000 could go towards the war. They deducted this amount when they voted an extraordinary supply (far less than was needed), so that by the autumn of 1689 the king was forced to borrow on the credit of future revenues and so was sucked into a vortex of debt. To add insult to injury, the Commons made no permanent provision for the revenue (although they extended the customs for another six months). William offered to produce accounts to show that nothing was being wasted and that he was desperately short of money. His offers were brushed aside with claims that they lacked the time to go through detailed figures and wild allegations of embezzlement and overspending.

William was furious. He 'said the Commons used him like a dog. Their coarse usage boiled so upon his stomach that he could not hinder himself from breaking out sometimes against them' [9 vol. II p. 21] [*Doc. 24*]. But there was little he could do: he could block measures he disliked, but he could not force the Commons to vote him money. To make matters worse, the enforced consensus of the early days of the Convention was over. Tories like Clarges vented their spleen on the man they saw as a usurper. Many Whigs were angry that William had denied them a monopoly of office. They especially resented his employing Nottingham, who had argued that the throne was not vacant, and devoted more energy to paying off old scores than to doing the king's business. Many backbenchers simply thought that they were being asked to vote too much in taxes. By the beginning of 1690, William had had enough. He dissolved the Convention and called a new parliament – which was to settle the revenue, but hardly to his satisfaction.

The settlement was thrashed out amid party rancour and allegations of mismanagement. William was voted the customs until 1694 (later extended to 1699 and then 1706). He was also given the temporary part of the excise for life: the remainder, being perpetual, he collected anyway. He was thus the first king since the fifteenth century (with the exception of Charles I) not to be granted the customs for life. Even if he had been, his ordinary revenue would have been much less than James II's. He had lost the hearth money and the French war diminished the yield of the customs. James's ordinary revenue averaged around one and a half million pounds; William's seldom yielded more than a million, sometimes less [74; 105; 107]. Moreover, so much of the ordinary revenue was applied to the war and it became so encumbered with debts that it was harder and harder to separate it from the extraordinary supplies voted specifically for the war. By 1698 the excise (intended mainly for the support of the civil government) was anticipated to the sum of £600,000 and half the customs revenue was appropriated for the navy. The war had destroyed the last traces of the idea that the ordinary revenue was an independent income for the king. In 1695–6 the Commons recognised this by arranging to borrow £515,000 for the civil expenditure, or civil list, and in 1697 they voted a supply of £515,000 for the same purpose. In 1698 William was voted a number of revenues for life, designed to bring in £700,000 a year, which was to cover the civil list: any surplus was to be applied to public purposes. It says much for his financial plight that he welcomed this arrangement [105].

Having distinguished between the civil and military elements in the Crown's ordinary expenditure, the Commons increasingly took over responsibility for military and naval expenditure, voting money to pay the interest on debts incurred on the various branches of the ordinary revenue. Under the pressures of war, the old distinction between ordinary and extraordinary revenue became so blurred as to be meaningless: some argued that the revenue 'is in the crown as a trust' and that 'what is given to the king . . . is not as he is king, but for support of the nation' [108 *p. 32*]. It was superseded by a more realistic distinction between civil and military expenditure. Such a distinction seemed particularly necessary in 1697–8, when many were unwilling to trust William with the army left over from the war, but it would probably have developed anyway. With the king given a revenue adequate only for his civil expenditure, the tradition that he should 'live of his own', which had received some mortal blows in 1689–90, was buried forever. From the reign of Anne, the monarch was voted the civil list for life, while the army and navy estimates were put before Parliament each year [74; 105].

The failure to grant William an adequate revenue in 1689–90 was deliberate [107]. 'If you settle such a revenue as that the king should have no need of a Parliament', said one MP, 'I think we do not our duty to them that sent us hither' [7 vol. X *p. 10*]. 'Granting it for life will prevent any ill ministers from being called in question', declared another [7 vol. X *p. 21*]. Dislike or distrust of William made the Commons determined not to surrender the financial weapon placed in their hands by the Revolution. They were concerned not only to curb the king's power, but also to investigate and punish the misdeeds of his ministers. Whatever the motives, the destruction of all hope of an independent royal revenue transformed the Crown's relationship with parliament. Now the Commons, if they chose, could force their wishes on the king by withholding supply. In practice, the picture was more complex, but the fact remains that the great constitutional change brought about by the Revolution owed far more to the impact of the financial settlement (compounded by the war) than to the change of ruler or the Bill of Rights.

6   THE RELIGIOUS SETTLEMENT

In 1640 there had been one Church in England and Wales to which all except Catholics nominally belonged, but there was much disagreement about its form. Much of the population seems to have accepted its religious provision with little question, if with varying degrees of enthusiasm, but two groups wished to change it. The first could be labelled Puritan. It harked back to the days of Elizabeth and James I, when the Church's theology had generally been seen as Calvinist, when many of its clergy placed preaching the Gospel above formal observance and ignored official requirements such as wearing a surplice or using the sign of the cross in baptism. The second could be called Arminian or Laudian (after Archbishop Laud). This came to prominence in the 1620s. It sought to restore elements of the pre-Reformation Church which some saw as valuable. Whereas Puritans denounced ceremonies and ritual as 'popish', Arminians argued that they served a valid spiritual purpose. They believed that Communion, not the sermon, should be the main focus of the service. They saw the priest as spiritually distinct from, and superior to, his flock, his distinctiveness emphasised by his consecrating the Communion bread and wine at the altar, now set at the east end of the church and railed off from the congregation. Their theology tempered stark Calvinist predestinarianism with a revived emphasis on free will.

This divergence of views on the Church was a major cause of the civil war. Resentment of Laudian innovation and the need for Scottish support led the Long Parliament to abolish bishops and forbid the use of the Prayer Book, but most English 'Presbyterians' (unlike their Scottish counterparts) had no dogmatic hostility to episcopacy. Their ideal remained the Church of Elizabeth and James. Most were willing to belong to an Episcopal Church, provided it was purged of Laudian innovations and representatives of the parish clergy were joined with the bishops in the Church's government. Most also had little quarrel with the Prayer Book, provided they were not forced to use those parts which they found distasteful.

The banning of the Prayer Book in the 1640s showed the strength of 'Anglican' sentiment (although the term was rarely used), as those who had quietly conformed now used the Book in defiance of authority. At the Restoration, Anglicans and Presbyterians agreed on the need to restore an effective parish-based national Church, but others did not. Since 1640 'gathered churches' had formed which ignored parish boundaries and were spiritually exclusive: only 'visible saints', the truly godly, were welcome. Whereas Anglicans and Presbyterians agreed that the Church should try to redeem sinners, the gathered Churches, buoyed up by hopes of an imminent Day of Judgement, saw no need to concern themselves with those soon to be consigned to hell-fire. They were to bring together the few who would be saved and seek God together. By 1660 the multiplicity of churches had mostly coalesced into sects – Independents (or Congregationalists), Baptists and Quakers.

The sects attracted only a small minority of the population – five per cent or less – and very few of the ruling elite, but their supporters were too numerous and committed to be easily suppressed. Both in 1660 and in 1689, there were two problems to be faced. First, that of 'comprehension': should the Church's liturgy and government be adapted to make them more palatable to Presbyterians? Should ministers be allowed some latitude on such matters as wearing the surplice? Should bishops share their authority with the parish clergy? Second, should the Church recognise that part of the population no longer wished to belong to any national Church and allow toleration (or 'indulgence') [117]?

At the Restoration, Parliament rejected both comprehension and indulgence. The Act of Uniformity of 1662 made no concessions to the Presbyterians: all parish clergy were to use the old Prayer Book (slightly revised) and swear their assent to all that it contained. Parliament also passed a series of Acts against non-Anglicans (now known as Dissenters or Nonconformists). Not only could they be punished severely for worshipping publicly, they were barred from public office.

The ruling elite had shown little enthusiasm for Laudianism in 1640, but much had changed. The young clergymen and gentlemen educated at the universities in the 1630s had grown up, so that there was now broader acceptance of what became known as 'High Church' values. High Churchmen regained control of the universities and passed on their views to another generation of ordinands and aristocrats. It would be misleading to see the Restoration Church as 'Laudian': the clergy preached far more than their Laudian predecessors. However, Laud's renewed emphasis on the Church's prescribed ceremonies was increasingly widely followed and in most churches the altar was again positioned at the east end [118].

The reasons for restoring the Church in its old form were not solely spiritual. Many linked the collapse of the old Church in 1640 to the subsequent collapse of social discipline and the traditional polity. The sects (especially the Quakers) had set the elite of the spirit against the traditional social elite, challenging the authority of squire and parson, turning the world upside-down. It was hoped that restoring a hierarchical, authoritarian Church would help to restore a hierarchical and authoritarian social order.

The rejection of comprehension and toleration in 1660–3 might have seemed final, but many refused to accept it. Charles tried several times to temper the rigidity of the Act of Uniformity and in 1672 granted indulgence to Dissenters. Within the Church, many disliked the High Churchmen's ritualism and 'persecuting temper'. These were prepared to subscribe to the Prayer Book, but sympathised with those who could not and hoped to accommodate moderate Presbyterians within the Church. In the Exclusion Crisis the importance of the Dissenting vote and the High Churchmen's commitment to James's cause led the Whigs to support both comprehension and indulgence, to unite Protestants against Popery. The failure of Exclusion, and the Tories' zest for revenge, brought a renewal of persecution in the early 1680s [118; 121].

James's unexpected decision to abandon the Anglicans and appeal to the Dissenters re-opened the question of toleration. High Churchmen who had urged severity against Dissenters suddenly claimed to see the error of their ways. Most argued that James's offers of toleration were insincere. Archbishop Sancroft and his bishops discussed possible reforms of the liturgy with leading Presbyterians. They countered James's tolerationist propaganda by denying that the Church favoured persecution, while Sancroft urged the parish clergy to greater diligence in looking after their flocks.

While the sincerity of these overtures may be doubted, they helped to thwart James's strategy of dividing Churchman from Dissenter. In a gesture of solidarity which would have been inconceivable in 1685, Dissenters visited the Seven Bishops in the Tower. Soon, however, the High Churchmen were as embarrassed by these overtures as the Tories were by their cautious welcome to William's invasion. It was one thing to build a common Protestant front against James, quite another to be faced with a foreign Calvinist king who clearly favoured Dissenters and distrusted High Churchmen. Anglicans blamed William for the destruction of the Episcopal Church in Scotland and feared that the same would happen to the Church of England: a Presbyterian address to William declared that they sought 'the terms of union wherein all the Reformed [Calvinist] churches agree'. By the beginning of 1689, the Church's leaders were having second thoughts about their promises to the Dissenters [*Doc. 25*]. They became still more uneasy and resentful when required to swear allegiance to William and Mary.

The heads of grievances had shown the support of a majority in the Commons for comprehension and toleration. The Churchmen countered by an attempt at damage limitation. After consulting a group of bishops, Nottingham introduced a comprehension and a toleration bill in the Lords; both received a second reading on 14 March 1689. The former offered less than a similar bill of 1680 and met with a cool response from the Dissenters, among whom only the Presbyterians had ever been interested in comprehension and more and more of these now preferred sectarian status to any form of comprehension that the Churchmen were likely to offer. On 16 March William polarised opinion further by urging the removal of the sacramental test for public office: under the Test and Corporation Acts all office-holders had to take Communion in an Anglican church. The suggestion was violently attacked by the Tories in the Commons; the Lords further reduced the concessions offered in the comprehension bill.

By the time the Lords' bill had passed and gone down to the Commons, a much more sweeping bill had been brought in by the radical Whig, John Hampden. A number of moderate Whigs, as well as the Tories, disliked this bill. Deadlock seemed likely, until William (as usual indirectly) offered a compromise, the essence of which was that the question of comprehension should be referred to Convocation, which was to meet in the autumn, and in the meantime the toleration bill should pass. That night a large meeting of Churchmen at the Devil tavern agreed to support this proposal. Only a minority of the members of the committee appointed to make recommendations to Convocation supported comprehension [*Doc. 26*]; it was not even discussed when Convocation met [69 Ch. 7; 74; 75; 117].

The vote at the Devil tavern showed that the Churchmen's first priority was to keep the Church's worship pure and uniform and to avoid the sin of schism. To achieve this, they were prepared to allow the toleration bill to pass, but they did so grudgingly. The Toleration Act made no mention of the virtues of tolerance, but stated prosaically that 'some ease to scrupulous consciences may be an effectual means to unite their majesties' Protestant subjects in interest and affection'. It repealed none of the laws against religious nonconformity, but exempted from the penalties of those laws all who were prepared to take the oath of allegiance and make the declaration against transubstantiation and other Catholic beliefs laid down in the 1678 Test Act. This allowed Protestant Dissenters (but not Catholics) to absent themselves from church and to worship freely, provided that the meeting place was notified to the civil or ecclesiastical authorities and that the doors were not locked. Dissenting clergymen were required to take the same oath and declaration and subscribe thirty-six of the Thirty-nine Articles. (Those which need not be taken related to homilies, the consecration of bishops and ministers and the authority of a national Church to impose ceremonies not prescribed by the Bible.) Baptists could omit the reference to infant baptism in Article XXVII. The Act even took account of the Quakers' refusal to take oaths. They were allowed to declare (rather than swear) that they denied the pope's authority and that they believed in the Trinity [2 *pp. 400–3*].

The Toleration Act was so drafted as to exclude from its benefits only Catholics, Socinians (who did not believe in the Trinity) and Jews. The Catholics apart (who could hardly hope for toleration so soon after James's reign) those excluded were very few indeed. In the range of denominations covered, the Toleration Act was without precedent, but Dissenters did not become fully equal to Anglicans. The universities were still closed to them. They still had to pay tithes and Church rates for the support of a Church to which they did not belong. Above all, they were excluded from municipal and other offices by the need to take Communion in order to qualify. Their attempts to circumvent these restrictions were to cause great controversy in the generation after 1689.

The Toleration Act was not the final humiliation for the High Anglicans. One reason why the Tories in the Commons were so hostile to comprehension was that the Whig majority insisted that the clergy take the oath of allegiance to William and Mary. Many could not in conscience do so, even though the oath was couched in the most neutral terms, as it involved breaking their oath of allegiance to James. Six bishops (including five of the seven who had petitioned James in 1688) and over four hundred of the lower clergy refused and were deprived of their benefices. Their departure was an unmitigated disaster for High Churchmen. It brought about the schism which the clergy had been so keen to avoid, while their steadfastness was an implied reproach to those who took the oaths. It enabled the Whigs to denounce the High Church clergy – and the Tories in general – as more loyal to James than to William. Finally, it accelerated the replacement of the High Church bishops appointed by Charles and James with more moderate men. The events of 1689 initiated a painful period of adjustment for the Church of England, and it is to the consequences of the Revolution settlement that we shall now turn.

PART THREE: THE POST-REVOLUTION ORDER

INTRODUCTION

Looking at the change of ruler, the Bill of Rights, the financial settlement and the Toleration Act, there seems little that was so dramatically new as to constitute a turning-point in English history, little that would merit the epithet 'Glorious' (or indeed, 'Revolution'). The significance of the change of ruler was limited and the Bill of Rights contained little that was new. Only the Toleration Act marked a clear break with what had gone before. And yet the Revolution changed English government and politics profoundly and irrevocably – more profoundly and irrevocably than the great upheavals of 1640–60. One cause of this was undoubtedly the financial settlement. The failure to grant William an adequate independent revenue was quite deliberate, but it was a pragmatic, almost devious way of preventing him from abusing royal power, which proved effective while raising no clear-cut issues of principle. Its effect was greatly accentuated by the French wars of 1689–97 and 1702–13. Both resulted directly from the Revolution and could well be described as wars of the English succession. When William came to England, the Dutch were already at war with France. It was natural that James should seek refuge there and that Louis XIV should take up his cause. War against France thus became a matter of survival: if England did not fight, James would return with a French army. Similarly, when James died in 1701, Louis recognised his son as James III, once again forcing England to join in a major continental war. These wars were on a scale England had never known before. They required unprecedented resources of men and money and imposed great strains on England's administrative and political institutions. These strains were unexpected, complex and also often interrelated, which makes it artificial to treat them separately. With these points in mind, let us consider the salient features of the post-Revolution order.

7 THE GROWTH OF THE STATE

One major change in Stuart England which was, until recently, little appreciated, was the growth of the state. Under James I and Charles I, the Crown employed few paid administrators, most of whom acquired their offices through patronage, inheritance or purchase and regarded them as pieces of property to be exploited to the utmost. Their salaries were small; most of their income came from fees charged to the public (as well as gifts or bribes). Many recognised that this was not a desirable system, but given the king's poverty there was no realistic alternative.

For the early Stuart Crown was financially underendowed. It subsisted on an odd mixture of revenues. Some stemmed from the king's own resources: he owned extensive estates, derived revenues from his position as head of the surviving vestiges of the feudal system and exploited some of his prerogative powers to raise money. In this sense, England was a 'domanial state', but the king also received revenue from taxation granted by Parliament: regularly from the customs and occasionally from the subsidy. This tax component in the royal revenues had two serious weaknesses. First, there were large areas of economic activity which effectively escaped tax: imports and exports were taxed, as was landed property, but goods bought and sold within the country usually were not. Secondly, the subsidy, from Elizabeth's reign onwards, was increasingly underassessed. Taxpayers returned estimates of their income, after deducting necessary expenses. They were not on oath, so they lied about their income. As the yield of a subsidy fell, the Commons voted two, four or even six, but never grasped the nettle of underassessment, so yields continued to fall.

This antiquated and inefficient fiscal system was drastically overhauled in the 1640s. On one hand, the king's personal and prerogative revenues were swept away. On the other, Parliament introduced two new taxes alongside the customs. The excise, on alcoholic drinks and other goods bought and sold within England, brought whole new areas of activity – and a large proportion of the population – into the tax system for the first time. The monthly assessment was a property tax which got round the problem of underassessment by fixing a quota which each county had to meet, so that if one person paid less, another would have to pay more [31].

The previous century had shown that the old fiscal system was inadequate to meet the escalating costs of war, but the Commons had been reluctant to vote too many taxes or to overhaul it. Now, Parliament had to raise as much money as possible as quickly as possible, in order to fight the king. The new taxes brought in far more than the old and the predictability of their yields provided good security for short-term loans. As a result, Parliament was able to build up the army and navy to a level which the early Stuarts could only have dreamed of.

Charles II inherited this modernised fiscal system. As we have seen, he was granted the customs and excise for life or in perpetuity, to which Parliament added the hearth tax. The Commons were also prepared, on occasion, to vote assessments: the £2,500,000 voted in 1664 was around six times larger than the six subsidies voted in 1628. This enabled Charles to keep up a modest army ('guards and garrisons') and a much increased navy, with three times as many substantial warships in 1662 as in 1642.

He and his ministers also benefited from, and sought to foster, an increased administrative professionalism which had developed since 1642. More civil servants received salaries and were appointed and promoted on merit: the latter was also true of naval officers. By the 1680s, all the major branches of the revenue were collected by salaried officials, who were carefully supervised and operated within a clearly defined hierarchy. Service to the state, or to the public, was beginning to replace the old proprietary view of office. Along with regularity in the methods of payment went regularity of bureaucratic routine: Pepys, with his obsession for neatness, order and method can be seen as a harbinger of a new era. Administrators began to use statistics systematically; the Treasury Commission of 1667 tried to impose some system on the chaos of royal spending; Sir George Downing tried to systematise government borrowing.

It was impossible to change overnight a system that was, in many ways, still that of the Middle Ages. The Exchequer continued to issue notched willow twigs (tallies) as receipts until the nineteenth century – but even these were used as instruments of short-term borrowing [52; 108]. Reliance on fees and gratuities (not to say bribes) had not disappeared, as Pepys's diary makes clear. Army commissions were bought and sold; colonels received a lump sum for their regiments, which encouraged them to falsify their muster rolls and cheat the soldiers.

The potential for a stronger state had been created by Parliament and could be fully exploited only with Parliament's co-operation. Where the Commons were prepared to co-operate, as in the grant of 1664, Charles II could deploy resources much greater than those of his predecessors, but such co-operation required trust and for much of his reign trust was lacking. Between 1689 and 1713, by contrast, whatever their differences on other matters, MPs, as in the 1640s, were committed to wars which they dared not lose and so had to finance those wars properly. At the same time, thanks to the financial settlement, they retained sufficient financial power over the king to prevent him from abusing his authority.

The wars of 1689–1713 saw a second, and decisive surge in the creation of what has been termed a 'fiscal-military' state [33; 100]. England became a major military, as well as a major naval, power, but without sacrificing traditional liberties, as often happened in 'absolute' monarchies on the continent. England's population was little more than one-quarter of that of France, but the fiscal transformation of the 1640s and the administrative developments of Charles II's reign created the potential to tap England's resources far more efficiently.

The process was not without its strain. In the war of 1689–97, England had to send large amounts of cash to supply the field armies in the Low Countries and pay subsidies to continental allies. This cash would normally have come from the surplus on the nation's overseas trade, but trade was badly disrupted by the war: naval convoys were insufficient and French privateers took a fearful toll. The export of specie depleted the stock of coin within England; what remained became so worn and clipped that its intrinsic value fell far short of its face value. The government's response, in 1696, was to call in the old coin, melt it down and issue new coins, with milled edges which could not be clipped. In the long run, this brought stability to the coinage, but the short-term impact of the recoinage was disastrous: a chronic shortage of coin, a virtual failure of remittances to the Low Countries and probably the most serious economic crisis of the century. It was sheer luck that England got through the war without an economic or financial collapse. It was also fortunate that in the war of 1702–13, when costs were very much heavier, trade held up extraordinarily well [68 Chapter by Jones; 80].

These economic problems heightened the political tensions of the 1690s. The army increased to 60,000 men (as large as the army of the Protectorate) leading to fears that William might use it to establish absolutism. The administrative departments which supplied and organised the armed forces grew too, as did the revenue administration. The Ordnance Office employed about 60 officers in 1683, 268 in 1692 and nearly 450 in 1704 [124]. By 1718 there were 561 full-time and around a thousand part-time customs officials in the port of London alone; Great Yarmouth had 46 full-time and 56 part-time customs men. Excise officials were, if anything, more numerous. New duties like the salt and leather taxes required hundreds of officials to collect them – about five hundred in the case of the latter [33; 103].

The great increase in the scale of government and in the amount of money it handled highlighted the effects of incompetence and increased the opportunities for corruption. Gentlemen who acted as land-tax officials were sometimes thousands of pounds in arrears. In the struggle between two rival East India companies in the 1690s, both sides resorted to large-scale bribery of politicians and civil servants.

Each case of corruption that came to light convinced MPs and the general public that much of the increased revenue from taxes passed illicitly into the pockets of civil servants and politicians, but the expansion of the executive seemed pernicious in another way. The peerage and gentry supplied the bulk of the membership of Parliament, dominated many small parliamentary boroughs and influenced numerous voters in the larger boroughs and the counties. The Crown had always had to enlist their co-operation if local government was to run smoothly. As Parliament became a more regular institution, their importance as MPs and electoral patrons became greater still.

In return for their co-operation, the Crown offered 'patronage'. Under the Tudors this might consist of grants of land, marriage to a royal ward or economic concessions, such as monopolies. Under the later Stuarts the predominant rewards were offices and pensions. With the expansion of the administration and the revenue, both became more abundant. Already under Charles II fears had been expressed that patronage – what became known as 'the influence of the crown' – might undermine the independence of the Commons to a point where it would no longer protest about corruption or abuses of the royal prerogative. After 1689, anxiety was expressed about the growing number of officials and military men in the Commons:

some categories were declared ineligible for membership, others were required to seek re-election. At a local level, the multiplication of revenue officials threatened to make them a significant, perhaps even a decisive, element in the electorates of many small boroughs: the greatest argument against Walpole's excise scheme of 1733 was that it would require so many new officials that they would take over the electoral system [89].

The fears that were so widely expressed about the growth of the Crown's patronage resources were not groundless. Politicians hoped to use the places at their disposal to build a following. As party rivalry intensified, offices became the objects of party competition. Party leaders pressed the monarch to give their followers a monopoly of office. However, a full-scale 'spoils system' (whereby offices were filled purely on political criteria) did not develop. Neither William nor Anne wished either party to have a monopoly of office, which would make the monarch a virtual prisoner of the party leaders. Many administrators resisted the pressure to turn their offices into political pawns. The new systems of promotion and supervision and the new ethos of professionalism militated against political interference, which could disrupt the smooth functioning of tax collection.

Other types of office were more amenable to exploitation as patronage. Sinecures persisted, especially in the older departments; so did the sale of commissions in the army. In the newer departments, formal routine and non-political appointments were most apparent at the lower levels: at the top, informal methods and political appointments remained common [124]. Even so, the growing professionalism of the expanding civil service helped it to cope with tasks different, qualitatively and quantitatively, from those of the past. After 1714, the pace of change slackened, but the structures and systems already in place adapted to the escalating financial demands of eighteenth-century warfare. Not until the mid-nineteenth century did the civil service undergo a transformation in terms of size, organisation and attitudes as profound as that of the Stuart period.

8   THE FINANCIAL REVOLUTION

As we have seen, after 1660, the Crown could levy permanent taxes on overseas trade and some areas of consumption at home and, if the need arose, Parliament would vote temporary taxes on land. These taxes were fiscally more efficient than the Crown's old feudal and prerogative revenues. They were also far less contentious and unpopular, for they had been voted by Parliament and did not depend on dubious interpretations of the law. As it turned out, the revenues granted to Charles II yielded so much that by the 1680s he no longer needed to call Parliament.

William's parliaments were careful not to give him sufficient to 'live of his own', but the trend towards more rational and efficient taxation of the nation's wealth continued. There were some new customs duties and many new excises. Taxation on land, traditionally imposed only in emergencies, became so frequent as to be permanent and the level of the land tax increased. Although the use of county quotas was abandoned and there was a return to individual assessment, this was much more accurate than in the past. Yields tended to become fixed: it could be predicted that a land tax of a shilling in the pound would bring in about half a million pounds, so that, as with the monthly assessment, its yield was substantial and predictable.

The Revolution accelerated a process which had begun in the civil wars and continued under Charles II, whereby the English became used to paying taxes. In France this was achieved largely by using soldiers to break the taxpayers' resistance, but this was not the case in England. Three reasons can be suggested for this. First, parliamentary consent to taxation meant that it was seen as legitimate. Second, experience of resistance led to the withdrawal of some taxes (such as the excise on meat), while others were levied in such a way as to minimise resistance [31]. Third, taxation became regular and predictable, a matter of routine. In the case of the land tax, yields became fixed and the fact that local notables supervised its assessment and collection made the increased amount and the increased frequency more bearable [35]. In the case of the excise, people became accustomed to the routine of search and inspection. By Anne's reign it was not uncommon for brewers to leave the key so that the excisemen could inspect the brewing if they were out.

All this made it possible for William III to levy vastly more in taxation than Charles I or Elizabeth. Charles I's average annual revenue was under one million pounds. James II's was around two million. William III's, between 1689 and 1697, was over three and a half million, with the land tax alone bringing in nearly two million; the average annual revenue between 1702 and 1713 was nearly six million. The level of taxation continued to rise sharply in each of the major wars of the eighteenth century, so that by the end of the century the English (contrary to their conviction that the French were taxed beyond endurance) were paying more in taxation than the French [52; 91].

As there was little inflation between Charles I's reign and Anne's, this massive increase in yield was a real one and it was achieved with the subject's consent, a consent expressed through Parliament and through those who administered the land tax at a local level. William III and his successors were more dependent on Parliament for money than any of his predecessors, but they were able to levy far more in taxation and to fight wars on a far larger scale. Co-operation with Parliament, enforced though it might be, proved much more lucrative than the limited financial independence of his predecessors. This co-operation, moreover, was not confined to taxation. It could also be seen in government borrowing and here, more than with taxation, the Revolution marked the start of a new era.

The inadequacy of the Crown's ordinary revenue, with money coming in slowly and unpredictably, forced kings to borrow to meet immediate needs, but until Charles II's reign Crown borrowing was haphazard and unsystematic. The king might levy forced loans, or fail to pay tradesmen's bills, or negotiate short-term loans with whoever could be persuaded to take the risk. The early Stuarts tended to put pressure to lend on those who were in some way vulnerable: foreign bankers, customs farmers or the City of London and East India Company (which could be threatened with the loss of their privileges). Lenders could not be sure that they would be repaid in full (or at all): much depended on whether they had friends at court. Tradesmen charged inflated prices, to allow for the probable delay or default in the payment of their bills. Such a lack of system and predictability made borrowing difficult and expensive.

The Interregnum saw the beginnings of a more rational system, helped by the fact that the yield of taxation was now more predictable and so offered lenders better security. Victuallers and other suppliers to the navy were prepared to advance more and more goods on credit. In addition, the growth of banking encouraged the habit – among landowners and civil servants as well as businessmen – of depositing their spare cash with a banker in return for interest. Charles II's government naturally targeted these bankers, together with others holding substantial amounts of cash (such as customs farmers and its own receivers of revenue, some of whom also acted as bankers). These were willing to advance money to the Crown, but only if the security was sufficient. Moreover, like other lenders, they needed flexibility. Faced with a sudden demand for cash, or a run on their reserves, they needed to be able to transfer the Crown debt they were holding to someone else – and not at a high discount [108].

In 1665 the Act for the Additional Aid of £1,250,000 (towards the Dutch War) tried to meet these needs. It laid down a procedure whereby the government could borrow (either directly or by delaying payments to government creditors) at 6 per cent. The orders authorising payment were to be numbered and paid in strict numerical order. Repayment became a matter of routine, not of personal favour, and the small investor could lend to the Crown and be confident of being repaid; this enhanced security made the orders much more readily transferable. Much of the benefit of this arrangement was lost when the Stop of the Exchequer of 1672 suspended the repayment of capital (although not the payment of interest) on the Exchequer's debts, and in the 1680s interest payments also fell seriously into arrears. Thus on the eve of the Revolution, the Crown's credit with both large and small investors was considerably shaken [52; 108].

With the French war and the inadequate provision for William's revenue, borrowing was essential. The government's indebtedness increased greatly, but there was no attempt like that of 1665 to re-organise its borrowing. Departments borrowed money as best they could, pressing suppliers to give extended credit and issuing Exchequer tallies or printed Treasury orders in return. Parliament soon accepted that the war was too expensive to be paid for out of current income and began to vote certain taxes, not to be spent directly on the war, but to pay interest on loans from the public or on debts already incurred. As few expected the war of 1689–97 to last as long as it did, the Commons concentrated on short-term rather than long-term borrowing. They also consistently overestimated the yields of the taxes they voted to service this borrowing, which made it hard to pay interest promptly and in full.

However, the very fact that Parliament now met annually for several months strengthened the credit of a system which depended substantially on anticipating the yield of future taxes. With Parliament's position secure, those taxes were more likely to be voted and collected. From 1692, the Commons listened more attentively to schemes for long-term borrowing. The interest on the 'tontine' loan of 1693 (in which surviving investors received more and more as others died off) was provided by excise duties voted for ninety-nine years. More important was the Tonnage Act of 1694. This provided for a loan of £1,200,000 at 8 per cent and for the subscribers to be incorporated as the Bank of England, empowered to deal in bills of exchange. The Bank's initial loan consisted of £100 'bills', for which it received Exchequer tallies. These bills added to the growing volume of negotiable paper and it soon began to issue banknotes as well in denominations as small as £5. The Bank was to prove invaluable as a means of attracting deposits from small investors which could then be lent to the government, but this system could not have worked without the confidence which stemmed from the Bank's resting on an Act of Parliament.

The tontine and the Bank were early signs of a system of credit resting on long-term borrowing, underpinned by Act of Parliament, rather than short-term borrowing through the anticipation of taxes and the delayed payment of government creditors. Under William, such long-term loans accounted for much less than half of the sixteen and a half million pounds borrowed during the French wars. The reliance on short-term expedients meant that the rate of interest was high – on average 8.3 per cent, at a time of stable prices. It was still a considerable achievement to borrow an average of some two million pounds a year (more than Charles II's average annual revenue) at a time when taxes were at an unprecedented level and the economy was disrupted by war and by the complete overhaul of the coinage.

Without this borrowing, which accounted for one-third of all expenditure in 1689–97, the war could not have been carried on. Mistakes were made, but the reign marked the start of a new era in British government finance, when war was paid for by borrowing as well as by taxation. Given the spiralling cost of warfare, this was the only way in which a comparatively small country like England could afford to fight larger countries like France. Gradually, it came to be accepted that the debts incurred in wartime were too large to be fully repaid when peace returned. The national debt, from being an embarrassment, came to be seen as permanent and a secure investment. Resting as they did on the credit of the nation, not the word of a king, government securities attracted investors from the continent as well as Britain. As it became easier to attract lenders, the rate of interest fell. Under Anne, Godolphin placed more emphasis on long-term annuities and less on short-term anticipations and used the Bank and the East India Company to attract larger loans from the public. Growing confidence in the government's credit, encouraged by military success, enabled him to increase the level of borrowing to an average of over two and a half million a year, while cutting interest rates to below 7 per cent. After the peace of 1713, interest rates fell steadily, to 3 per cent or less in the 1730s. Pride in this achievement was captured in a pamphlet of 1733:

> There can't be a stronger proof of that high esteem which the people of England, and the neighbouring nations also, entertain for our glorious constitution than the immense credit our legislature has found in borrowing of money. It is not probable that the greatest absolute monarch could, in his most extensive dominions, raise by voluntary contributions a loan of fifty millions of money. And yet France, Turkey, Persia, India and China severally yield much larger annual revenues than Great Britain. [*52 p. 16*]

The Glorious Revolution marked a turning-point in the government's ability to raise money and to wage war, which reflected an increase in both tax revenue and borrowing. The war of 1689–97 cost about five and a half million pounds a year, that of 1702–13 about eight and a half million, that of 1756–63 about twenty-three million. In each case about one-third of the cost was met by borrowing and two-thirds from taxation [52]. This had two major consequences. First, Britain became a major European and world power. Henry VIII's reign had shown that England was a second-class power. In the 1520s his mounting demands for taxation provoked a taxpayers' strike. In the 1540s, wary of provoking the taxpayers again, he financed his wars by selling off vast tracts of monastic land (thus wasting a golden opportunity to achieve an adequate financial foundation) and by ruinous debasements of the coinage. Elizabeth defeated the Spanish armadas with the help of a large measure of luck and took nine years to suppress a rebellion in Ireland. The Cadiz and La Rochelle fiascos showed that Charles I lacked the financial resources to fight a major war.

After 1689, the contrast was enormous. Anne's armies ranged from the Netherlands to Bavaria and Spain. England became the prime mover of the coalition against France. This dramatic change in England's European role was made possible only by the dramatic improvement in the government's ability to raise money, which in turn was made possible only by the Crown's ability to win the nation's co-operation, through Parliament and financial institutions like the East India Company and the Bank.

The second major consequence of the 'financial revolution' stemmed from the growth of these financial institutions. The fact that they could mobilise such vast sums gave them a potentially huge political influence. It was widely feared that they might hold the government to ransom by cutting off the flow of loans. The Bank's directors tried to exert such pressure in 1710, in an effort to prevent Godolphin's dismissal, but they failed and Harley built up the South Sea Company as an alternative source of loans. In fact, fears of the great corporations' malign political influence proved exaggerated.

There was more substance to complaints of the rise of the 'monied interest'. The vast increase in government borrowing meant that bankers and financiers prospered. Some became enormously and ostentatiously rich and bought their way into Parliament. In the past, most successful businessmen, having made their fortunes, had bought country estates and sought to merge into the gentry. Many of the new monied men did not. Land was taxed heavily, agricultural prices were sluggish and rents were low, while land prices were high, so there was little economic incentive for *nouveaux riches* to buy land. Many landowners found it hard to find satisfactory tenants and wrote off rent arrears in bad years. They thus found it particularly galling that men of humble or even immigrant origins (Huguenots or Netherlanders) were becoming so rich that they could outbid country gentlemen for the support of the electorate, while landowners struggled to maintain their standard of living. Many claimed that the wars were part of a great conspiracy whereby money was transferred, via the land tax and government borrowing, from the landowners to the monied men [*Doc. 27*].

Before 1688 England's society and government were dominated by landowners, their temporary eclipse in the 1640s and 1650s making them doubly determined to reassert what they saw as their rightful primacy. One key to the landed elite's continued dominance was its willingness to absorb new wealth acquired elsewhere: the parvenus of one century became the established county families of the next. What was so obnoxious about the new monied men was partly the extent of their wealth, partly their unwillingness to be absorbed, to recognise that social status could not be attained without land. For a while it seemed that the landowners' dominance over government and society was in jeopardy and this sense of threat explains the bitter attacks on the monied men in Anne's reign. The return of peace meant a cut in the land tax and a halt to government borrowing, while the circle of those investing in government funds widened to include many landowners. The animosities of Anne's reign died down, the great financial institutions came to be accepted as part of the natural order. By the mid-eighteenth century the monied men had been quietly absorbed into a ruling class that was once more united and self-confident. This process of absorption can be seen in the case of Samson Gideon, who enjoyed great influence in government circles in the 1750s, despite being not only a financier but also a Jew. His son became a Christian and an Irish peer.

9 RELIGION AFTER THE REVOLUTION

The Toleration Act recognised the existence of the religious pluralism which had been a fact of life since the 1640s. The Churchmen allowed it to pass as the price of killing the comprehension bill: they maintained the purity of their Church's worship, but increased the numbers permanently outside it. Yet if dissent from the established Church was now legally permissible, the Church remained established. After 1689 the Church gradually lost the practical benefits of its established status. While other denominations could adapt their organisation or liturgy at will, the Church of England could do so only with Parliament's approval: to create a new parish required an Act of Parliament.

The benefits which the Church retained in 1689 turned out to be more apparent than real. The Act required everyone to attend either their parish church or a licensed meeting house, but this proved unenforceable. Many attended neither and church attendance fell sharply. The Church courts, restored with reduced powers at the Restoration, had continued to harass nonconformists and to punish moral offences under Charles II. Now their powers became still more attenuated and they dealt mostly with matters relating to the clergy and the fabric of parish churches. As the Toleration Act made no provision for checking on the orthodoxy of schoolteachers, the Church lost its monopoly of education, except at university level. Even there its advantages were eroded in practice, as the two English universities subsided into a complacent intellectual torpor. Student numbers fell, while the Dissenting academies became renowned for their academic vigour. Perhaps the Church's greatest advantage after 1689 was the Anglican monopoly of public office and political power, but this was undermined by occasional conformity: many Dissenters took Communion in an Anglican church once a year to qualify for office.

For Churchmen who had insisted so loudly on uniformity in the 1660s and early 1680s, the loss of the Church's position of supremacy came as a profound shock. Worse was to follow. The lapsing of the Licensing Act in 1695 destroyed the last vestige of clerical control over the press. The end of censorship was followed by a small flurry of publications which advocated deism or even atheism. Locke claimed that the only belief essential to salvation was that Jesus was the Messiah. Among the clergy, Samuel Clarke did not believe in the Trinity. Benjamin Hoadly claimed that God required only that one should be sincere in one's beliefs: He had laid down no dogmas or doctrines. Any church was as good as any other – indeed, there was no need for churches at all. For High Churchmen it was intolerable that a man with such beliefs should be an Anglican priest, but Hoadly prospered mightily, thanks to the patronage of Whig politicians, who relished Hoadly's quasi-Lockean political tracts almost as much as his baiting of High Churchmen. He ended his days in the plum bishopric of Winchester [120].

Churchmen tried hard to re-establish a measure of control. Parliament passed a Blasphemy Act in 1698, but it proved difficult to convict the authors of 'blasphemous' works. To many, these were symptomatic of a collapse of traditional spiritual and moral values, seen also in occasional conformity (prostituting the Church's sacraments to gain office) and the lewdness of stage plays. There was a widespread conviction that crime and immorality were out of control. London magistrates ordered those seen as 'loose, idle and disorderly' – prostitutes, drunks, gamesters and those with no visible means of support – to be sent to the house of correction, where they were whipped and put to a few days' hard labour [113]. Societies for the Reformation of Manners laboured to identify and prosecute these same vicious and disorderly elements [48]. But all their efforts were insufficient to stem the tide.

The 1690s seemed a time of brash innovation and financial projects; fortunes were made overnight by dubious means, such as gambling on stocks and shares; public life was riddled with bribery and corruption. Nothing was taken for granted or immune from questioning. Such an atmosphere – amoral, experimental and metropolitan – was profoundly alien to traditional Anglicans. Their values were those of village society, where the squire-magistrate and parson enforced traditional Christian morality and the peasants came to church each Sunday to be taught their duties. But now (except where there was a diligent resident squire) they could no longer be made to come to church or to heed its teachings: as the

Churchmen became angrier, so they came to blame all the ills of society on the Church's loss of coercive power and on the Toleration Act. Many would have liked to repeal the Act: far more wished at least to plug its most obvious loopholes, by banning occasional conformity and those 'nests of sedition', Dissenting schools.

The contrast between London and the country had always existed but had never seemed so stark as in the 1690s. As Dissenters went into open competition with the Church and circumvented the law to break the Anglicans' monopoly of office, as jumped-up immigrant bankers made huge fortunes while taxes rose, agriculture languished and foreign trade was disrupted by the wars, as atheism and immorality seemed to flourish unchecked, the Churchmen's resentment grew into a deep, bitter anger. Their standpoint might be reactionary, but they spoke for much of the population of the villages and small towns where most English people lived. Even in London, the Tories won much support: under Anne they had a majority on the annually-elected common council and came close to winning a majority on the court of aldermen as well [49]. The Churchmen had the great asset of speaking for tradition in a conservative society and of an ideal of the social order which still bore some resemblance to reality and which appeared all the more perfect in comparison with an unappealing present [28; 55] [*Doc. 29*].

The Churchmen's discomfiture under William was compounded by their own divisions. The High Church element was the largest. Since 1660 the universities had turned out hundreds of High Church parsons and imbued the sons of the gentry with similar principles. They believed that the Church of England was the one Church that was both Catholic and Reformed. They stressed its continuity with the pre-Reformation Church, through the maintenance of wholesome ceremonies, the central place given to Holy Communion and its unbroken succession of bishops. After 1660 episcopacy came, more than ever, to be seen as the only divinely ordained form of Church government, so the Church's episcopal government marked it off from both Dissenters and most foreign Protestant Churches [118]. The High Church clergy and laity had provided much of the impetus and ideology of the Tory reaction of the 1680s. When James II forced them to choose between the twin pillars of their ideology – Church and king – most chose to obey God rather than man. While still proclaiming that active resistance to the king could never be justified, they insisted that it was wrong to obey royal commands which would lead to the destruction of God's Church

[55; 59]. Horrified by the events of the winter of 1688–9, High Churchmen again proclaimed their commitment to legitimism and non-resistance and took the oaths to the new rulers reluctantly, if at all. Some claimed that they had taken them only in order to carry on the fight against those they saw as the Church's enemies – the Low Churchmen and Latitudinarians.

These two elements within the Church were often lumped together, but should be distinguished. The Low Church proper represented a continuation of the moderate, evangelical Puritan tradition of the reigns of Elizabeth and James I, which had found a home among the Presbyterians of the 1640s and 1650s. Its spirit was expressed by clergymen like Ralph Josselin (who conformed under Charles II, but almost never wore a surplice) and Richard Baxter, who refused to conform, but never regarded himself as a Dissenter and had more in common with most Low Churchmen than with doctrinaire Presbyterians. Low Churchmen wanted a simple service, uncluttered by ceremonies, and with the main emphasis on preaching the Word [*Doc. 28*].

The Latitudinarians were products of a newer intellectual climate. Low Churchmen maintained the traditional Christian emphasis on human frailty and depravity. Man fought a constant losing battle against his own sinful nature and could not begin to understand God's complex and inscrutable purposes. All he could do was follow God's word, literally, as set out in the Bible. The Latitudinarians' outlook reflected both increased confidence in human potential and weariness with wranglings about Biblical texts. Advances in science made some wonder if man really was such an insignificant blemish on the face of creation. Copernicus and Galileo, Newton and Harvey, showed that the universe and the human body seemed to function according to ascertainable laws. Phenomena which had once seemed the work of a severe and vengeful God were now explained, and the belief grew that others, still inexplicable, would one day be understood. God receded from the foreground: instead of intervening constantly in earthly affairs, he had set in motion a marvellously complex set of mechanisms which functioned independently.

The Latitudinarians argued that one should seek to deduce the basic moral precepts which underlay the elaborate rules of conduct of the Old Testament. To them, God no longer appeared a demanding tyrant, but the benevolent architect of a rational universe, in which man should use his own reason. The emphasis in moral theology changed, from an obsession with sin and human inadequacy to a simple, prudential morality. To live a good life was easy, pleasant and profitable. Such an outlook had no place for the torments of hell, for the agony of doubt or, indeed, for strong emotions of any kind. So concerned were the Latitudinarians to avoid 'enthusiasm' that they made religion bland to the point of dullness [*Doc. 30*].

The opposition to High Churchmen within the Church of England thus consisted partly of old-style Puritans and partly of new-style Latitudinarians. By the early eighteenth century the latter were far more influential than the former and were becoming known, confusingly, as Low Churchmen. They agreed with traditional Puritans in placing little emphasis on ceremonies and a tolerant attitude towards Dissenters, accepting the Toleration Act as an accomplished fact, which could not (and should not) be changed.

In seeking to rebuild the Church's power, the High Churchmen faced an uphill task. Most bishoprics under William and Anne went to Low Churchmen, Latitudinarians or moderates. William's sympathies were Calvinist and he and Mary resented the High Churchmen's reluctance to recognise them as 'rightful and lawful' monarchs. Anne was a devout Anglican, but turned against the High Churchmen after they threatened, in 1704, to hold up the money needed for the war in order to force through a bill against occasional conformity. Only one rabid High Churchman, Atterbury, became a bishop between 1689 and 1714. The rest were mostly, in Burnet's words, 'men both of moderate principles and of calm tempers' [3]. If the Church was to speak with their voice, the High Church clergy had first to impose their wishes on the bishops and this led to the demand for the recall of Convocation [*Doc. 29*].

Convocation was the clerical equivalent of Parliament. The Upper House consisted of the bishops, the Lower of representatives of the lesser clergy. In 1689, the Lower House proved so intractable that William decided that it should never meet again, but in the later 1690s High Churchmen pressed for its recall. Lay politicians whose support William needed in order to manage Parliament (notably Rochester) insisted that it should meet, as a condition of their accepting office. From 1701 to 1717 it met each year. The bishops used various methods to delay proceedings in the Lower House. Although some useful ecclesiastical business was conducted, the High Churchmen's attempts to use Convocation as a political weapon were largely unsuccessful [28; 72].

The High Churchmen were more successful in elections and in the Commons. Under Anne, religion once again became a major political issue. In the last years of her reign, an overwhelmingly Tory Commons secured the passing of Acts against occasional conformity and Dissenting schools. On a more constructive note, Churchmen founded the Society for the Propagation of Christian Knowledge, opened charity schools (to teach religion to the children of the poor) and were initially active in the Societies for the Reformation of Manners (although these came to be dominated by Dissenters). Acts were passed establishing funds to enhance clerical stipends and to build fifty new churches in the environs of London: only twelve were built, albeit on a grand scale.

The High Churchmen under Anne were both militant and dynamic. It was not to last. After the Whigs regained power in 1714, the Acts against occasional conformity and Dissenting schools were repealed. Convocation ceased to meet. The Tories became an impotent minority in the Commons. All the top posts in the Church went to Whigs, including the obnoxious Hoadly. High Church values survived, at Oxford and in many parishes, but had no influence in the upper reaches of the Church. Latitudinarianism had triumphed. While many priests and laymen showed sincere, if undemonstrative, piety, this was a Church without strong emotions. It advanced into the eighteenth century, eschewing enthusiasm, its top posts the objects of political patronage [120].

DISSENT

As we have seen, the Church was adversely affected by the Toleration Act, but this does not mean that Dissent prospered. The number of Dissenters probably increased in the quarter century after 1689. The most sophisticated estimate [126] suggests a figure of about 350,000 in 1715–18, or just over 6 per cent of the population. Of these, just over half were Presbyterians, followed by Independents (or Congregationalists) and Baptists (each with a little over 60,000) and about 40,000 Quakers. The geographical incidence of Dissent varied, according to the denomination. Presbyterianism was strong in some areas where Church Puritanism had been strong, such as the south-west (apart from Cornwall), Lancashire, Cheshire and Essex, also Northumberland where the Scots influence may have been significant. With the exception of Carmarthenshire, it made little impact in Wales, where the Church had traditionally been weak and where Independents and Baptists made far more of an impact, mainly in the south. In England, the Independents and Baptists were strongest in the east Midlands and south-east and made little impact in the north. The Quakers had very little following in Wales, the South-west or the extreme southern counties; elsewhere they were quite evenly spread, with larger concentrations in Cumbria, the counties to the north and east of London and above all Bristol [126].

The brief flurry of expansion after 1689 was soon over. By the 1730s all denominations were suffering a decline in numbers. Evangelical movements have always shown a tendency to run out of steam. It is hard to sustain the commitment which stems from the initial excitement of conversion. As numbers grow, emphasis shifts from expansion to consolidation. Wealthy adherents wish to invest their money and effort, not in new missionary efforts, but in new chapels. There are disputes about doctrine or organisation, within or between denominations. There are fewer new recruits, while old adherents (and, still more, their children) fall away. Such processes could be seen in English Dissent in the early eighteenth century. The Presbyterians, after the failure of comprehension in 1689, finally became resigned to sectarian status. More and more moved away from their Calvinist roots towards heterodoxy, especially on the Trinity. They lost many of their less educated, more traditionally minded adherents and became the most intellectual of Dissenters. Indeed, they eventually lost all connection with old-style Presbyterianism and became Unitarians [29].

While the Presbyterians abandoned their Puritan roots, others clung to them more closely. Independents and Baptists became increasingly inward-looking and rigid, abandoning the evangelism and flexibility of their formative years for an obsession with doctrinal correctness. The Quakers shed their initial aggression and exhibitionism and subsided into a quietist respectability, whose chief effect was a continual dwindling of numbers. Thus, while Latitudinarianism dominated the Church of England, Old Dissent subsided into blandness or introspection. The fire of the Puritanism of the first half of the seventeenth century was revived only by the Methodists, who rediscovered the drama and anxiety of faith, conversion and redemption.

To many in the mid-eighteenth century, Methodism seemed a throwback to an earlier age. Wesley was unusual among educated men in seeing everything in the Bible as the Word of God (and in believing in witches). By the mid-eighteenth century most people had come to see religion as a private matter. The Latitudinarian emphasis on the basic essentials of Christianity had triumphed over the dogmatic, intolerant certainties of High Churchman and Puritan alike. Even the Catholics seemed less dangerous after the failure of the Jacobite rebellion of 1745. In practice, they could worship as they wished and 1791 saw the first tentative step towards Catholic emancipation.

It would be naive to see the Toleration Act as the sole reason for this new tolerance. Clearly it was a product of long-term intellectual developments. Nevertheless, the fact that the Act had been passed strengthened the position of the advocates of toleration. Despite the Churchmen's warnings, toleration did not lead to civil war or anarchy. The reasons for passing the Act were practical rather than ideological, yet belief in the principle of toleration, which had existed well before 1689, was strengthened by the simple fact that toleration now existed and could be seen to work. Again pragmatism emerges as the salient feature of the Glorious Revolution.

10 THE CONSTITUTION: CROWN AND PARLIAMENT

As we have seen, the Declaration of Rights was in many ways a limited and conservative document. Its main concern was to prevent a recurrence of the misgovernment of Charles II and James II. Only in a negative sense did it define the future relationship of Crown and Parliament. The more novel proposals contained in the Heads of Grievances were dropped before the Declaration was read to William and Mary. The evolution of the post-Revolution constitution owed far less to the Bill of Rights than to the Crown's new financial weakness and to the unprecedented administrative, financial and political strains created by the French wars. As a result of these new conditions, the relationship of Crown and Parliament developed in a way that few could have predicted in 1689. Parliament now met each year, for several months. The royal prerogative, for so long a potential threat to liberty and property, was now effectively curbed. Meanwhile, the growth of the executive and of the revenue created the possibility that the Crown might be able to control Parliament by means of places and pensions. The 'influence' of the Crown thus came to seem a greater threat than the prerogative to the integrity of Parliament and the well-being of those it represented. This threat was never entirely realised, but under George I and II skilful use of the Crown's patronage was a major factor in the successful management of Parliament.

The Crown's continued success in managing Parliament obscures a change of fundamental importance. By George II's reign, the king's personal role in government was much smaller than in the seventeenth century. It was now the king's ministers who controlled the administration, managed Parliament and exploited the Crown's patronage; although they owed their places in part to the king's favour, the king's choice was limited to men who could manage the Commons. The relationship of king and Commons had changed more than was at first apparent, but the most profound change lay in the relationship between king and ministers, between the king and the politicians.

The post-Revolution period saw new statutory restrictions on the Crown, mostly reflecting experience of William's reign rather than implementing the programme of 1689. The king's freedom to call and dismiss Parliament was curtailed by the Triennial Act of 1694, which reflected fears of the 'influence of the Crown'. The Triennial Acts of 1641 and 1664 had been concerned to ensure that Parliament met at least once every three years. Now that Parliament met annually, concern shifted to the danger that a long-standing Parliament might be corrupted by the misuse of patronage. Under the 1694 Act there was to be a general election at least once every three years: in fact, there were ten in the next twenty years and the country remained almost continually in the grip of election fever. This Act was repealed by the Septennial Act of 1716, under which a Parliament could remain in being for seven years. The other major piece of restrictive legislation was the Act of Settlement of 1701. This vested the succession (after Anne) in the House of Hanover, but the mainly Tory House of Commons showed its dislike of William and of the prospect of another foreign king by laying down various restrictions which were to come into force when Anne died. These showed a mixture of xenophobia (as with the prohibition on foreigners' holding office) and suspicion of the influence of the Crown (as with the exclusion of all office-holders from Parliament) [*Doc. 31*].

Of the legislative proposals in the 'heads of grievances' of 1689, few reached the statute book. The prohibition of the monarch's marrying a Catholic was included in the Bill of Rights. Acts were passed in 1689 for toleration (but not comprehension) and a new coronation oath. Of the rest, the Triennial Act prevented the 'too long continuance' of any Parliament; an Act of 1696 regulated treason trials; and the judges' tenure was changed by the Act of Settlement, so that they could no longer be dismissed without Parliament's consent. (This harked back to James II's purges of the judiciary: William had not put pressure on his judges.) The Act of Settlement also declared that a royal pardon could not save a person from impeachment, an item included in the first draft of the 'heads of grievances' but not the final version. It was incorporated in the Act of Settlement because the Tories hoped to impeach William's Whig ministers. For the rest, the demands for the abolition of the hearth tax and for frequent sessions of Parliament were rendered irrelevant by events. Attempts to stamp out electoral corruption and to reform the legal system bore little fruit. The Elections Act of 1696 said nothing of bribery or treating and concentrated mainly on sheriffs' malpractices. With William showing no inclination to pervert the electoral and legal systems, the twin forces of inertia and vested interest were sufficient to prevent change. Besides, these old problems seemed less pressing as new and more urgent issues arose [69 Ch. 1; 74; 110].

The restrictions imposed by statute on the prerogative were limited. The king still had the power to call and dismiss Parliament at will (subject to the Triennial, or Septennial, Act), to choose his ministers, to direct the administration and to formulate policy. Most of these powers still belong to the Crown in theory, but in practice monarchs have found it more and more difficult to exercise them. One of the peculiarities of the British constitution is the great difference between the Crown's theoretical and actual powers. This difference was the product of financial and political pressures which developed from 1689. These imposed limitations on the Crown (some embodied in 'conventions', some not) far more constricting than those imposed by statute. The crucial factor was the Crown's financial dependence on Parliament. MPs had long talked of 'redress before supply', the need for grievances to be redressed before money was granted. Before 1640 the Crown had had far too many independent sources of revenue for such demands to be effective. Even under Charles II, the king's financial position was seldom so desperate that he had to succumb to such pressures.

After 1689, however, MPs knew they possessed the financial power to get their way. William knew it too. He avoided measures which might antagonise the Commons, while politicians sometimes used the threat of blocking supply in an effort to intimidate him. In 1690, Halifax noted that William 'said he would not have the bill of corporations pass. Said that some of the party that pressed it had sent him word that if he interposed or meddled in it, they would not finish the money bills' [9 vol. II p. 243]. More blatant was the practice of 'tacking' clauses on other matters to money bills. By tradition, the Lords could not amend money bills, so the Lords and king had to choose between passing such bills (complete with the 'tacked' clauses) or rejecting them and depriving the king of supply. Tacking was clearly seen as a last resort, to be used where reasoned argument had failed, but it was none the less regarded as justifiable. 'Since it can be no otherwise done,' declared Paul Foley in 1694, 'we must tack our grievances to our money bills; for we have just fears and grievances as long as we have a standing army' [7 vol. X p. 382].

This remark was made during debates on William's vetoing a triennial bill, during which some speakers effectively denied the king's right of veto. Robert Harley claimed that bills had rarely been vetoed in the past, especially when an abundant supply had been granted. 'One of the greatest crimes the minister can be guilty of is to persuade the king not to pass bills,' he said [7 vol. X. *p. 368*]. Such remarks and the occasional use of tacking show that the Commons knew that they had the financial power to reduce the king to a cipher, if they used it systematically. But they did not. The threat in 1690 to withhold supply unless William dropped his opposition to the corporation bill came to nothing. Tacking was used only when a majority of MPs felt that it was absolutely necessary, that the Lords and king were opposing the Commons' wishes unreasonably. It was an occasional, almost desperate tactic, not a regular practice. The Lords disliked it, and if the Commons used it excessively the Lords were likely to delay or obstruct business which was important to the Commons. The king, too, could retaliate by using his veto.

Such practical considerations apart, many MPs had reservations about the propriety of tacking. Although they knew that their 'power of the purse' enabled them to force their wishes on the king, they lacked the will or the cohesion to use that power systematically. It is tempting to treat the Commons as an organism with a single mind and purpose. In fact, it comprised some five hundred individuals with varying interests and aptitudes. Some were concerned with local prestige or local economic interests, some were eager to solicit rewards for themselves and their kinsmen, but only a minority were interested in a 'political career'. MPs were unpaid. Long, regular sessions were a novelty which many disliked. Most still saw government as the king's business. They did not want the responsibility of policy making and administration. They wanted to criticise what they saw as errors of policy or maladministration, especially where their class or personal interests were affected. They wanted, also, to criticise the misdeeds of ministers and courtiers and (in some cases) to thrust themselves forward as replacements.

Such complaints and criticisms were essentially selective. MPs criticised particular policies and particular ministers. They attacked the misuse of executive authority but not the king's right to direct the executive, because they did not want executive responsibilities themselves. Late in 1689, after allegations of gross abuses in the provisioning of the army in Ireland, William asked the Commons to name men to take over the job and to report on the state of the Irish forces. The House was embarrassed. One MP said 'it was not the practice of your ancestors to recommend persons for the executive part. The king's council and generals are fittest, knowing the abilities and qualities of persons' [7 vol. IX *p. 473*]. The House asked to be excused from nominating anyone and referred everything to 'His Majesty's great wisdom'. As Sir Edward Seymour explained a few days later: 'We have no part of the executive authority of the government, but we may advise the king. ... The general scheme of the state of the nation is as much as we can represent to the king. ... It is not in our power to remedy the miscarriages, but it is to represent them to the king to be remedied' [7 vol. IX *pp. 488–9*].

The Commons did not normally use their financial position to wrest power from the king, but did so if a sufficiently large majority felt sufficiently angry to exert sustained financial pressure. The growth of parties threatened to change this. While the Commons remained an agglomeration of individuals or small groups, it was hard to keep a majority together on any but the most emotive issues. The development of party issues and the use of party discipline gave the leaders of the majority party the opportunity to force their way into office: if the monarch would not employ them, they could make the House unmanageable. Taken to its logical extreme, this would have turned the monarch into the tool of the party leaders. Between 1705 and 1710 the Whig leaders used their control of the Commons to force Anne to dismiss her Tory advisers, to admit Whigs to office and to follow Whig policies [*Doc. 33*]. In 1707 she had to resort to subterfuge to appoint two moderate Tory bishops. After 1715 the constant Whig majority in the Commons left the first two Georges with no choice but to appoint Whig ministers.

The Crown's position was not as desperate as it seemed. There were limits to how far politicians could carry their obstruction: if they took it to the point of jeopardising the war effort, their followers might desert them. Not all politicians were fervent party men. Some great ministers, like Marlborough, Godolphin, Harley and Sunderland, put service to the Crown before party. Career civil servants like William Lowndes served under ministries of any party complexion. Among the party men, some moderates, like the Duke of Somerset, were prepared to serve in mixed ministries. The party leaders were rarely so united that the Crown could not play one off against another or rely on moderates rather than extremists – the Whig Junto's solidarity in 1705–10 was exceptional. After 1715 the Whigs' supremacy was so secure that they felt little need for unity. Had George I and II been more astute, their choice of possible ministers would have been wider than it was [70].

After 1689, the king's financial weakness gave the Commons the power to impose their will on him, if they chose to do so. He was commander-in-chief of the armed forces, but in 1697–8 William was forced to reduce the army to what he saw as suicidally small proportions. The king formulated foreign policy, but Parliament had to pay for war. Like his predecessors, William generally tried to keep Parliament (and his ministers) ignorant of some of his negotiations. After the Commons expressed outrage, in 1701, on discovering the secret partition treaty of 1698, William was careful to keep the House informed and ask its advice. Finally, as we have seen, the monarch's right to choose his ministers, still respected in theory, proved harder and harder to exercise in practice. MPs' suspicions of corruption and mismanagement could be exploited by politicians eager to do down their rivals. Even William reluctantly acknowledged the need to appoint ministers who could manage Parliament, even if he disliked them personally. Like Sunderland, he came in 1693–4 to accept that 'whenever the government has leaned to the Whigs it has been strong, whenever the other has prevailed it has been despised', even though he also agreed that 'the Whigs make me weary of my life' [86 *p. 251*].

Such pressures led to the decline of personal monarchy. William possessed exceptional ability and determination. His control of foreign policy was facilitated by his being able to use the Dutch diplomatic service. Relying on a few comparatively humble officials, he directed, almost single-handed, the administration of the army and, to a lesser extent, the navy. Yet even William, with all the prestige he enjoyed as England's saviour in 1688 and as the leader of the coalition against France, suffered numerous defeats and humiliations [*Doc. 16*]. Political needs forced him to appoint men he despised – he would not even speak to Lord Wharton. Parliament rescinded his grants of Irish lands to Dutchmen and Huguenots, with cutting remarks about the rapacity of foreigners. Worst of all, William was forced to disband most of the army at a time when he believed that a renewal of the war was imminent, and to send home his Dutch guards [23].

Anne has perhaps been underestimated by historians. If she lacked William's exceptional gifts, she was conscientious and determined, with clear views of her own. Her main concern was to win the war. She wished to maintain the toleration of 1689 while preventing further weakening of the Church. She was also determined to preserve the Crown's prerogatives and to avoid domination by party politicians [*Doc. 32*]. She clung to these principles in the face of ruthless and cynical pressure from those (not least the Duchess of Marlborough) who sought to take advantage of her sex and physical frailty [*Doc. 33*]. Despite her efforts, her abilities were inferior to William's and she faced greater problems, with the intensification of party rivalries. As a result her defeats, especially at the hands of the Whig Junto, were more numerous [61].

George I and George II were less able than Anne. George I's resentment of the 'Tory' peace of 1713 and his acceptance of the Whig equation of Toryism and Jacobitism left him no choice but to rely on the Whigs, but the Whigs were not united. It said much for Walpole's skill as both a court and a parliamentary politician that he monopolised the two kings' favour for twenty years. His security of tenure and the Georges' mediocrity made it possible to carry on the government with less reference to the king's personal wishes. Decisions reached in cabinet were presented to the king as *faits accomplis*. Walpole extracted the maximum of political benefit from the Crown's patronage and pursued policies at home and abroad that were designed to be congenial to independent backbench MPs. This mixture of patronage and policies gave Walpole a well-nigh unshakable hold on the Commons, which greatly strengthened his hand in dealing with the king [89; 103].

Ministers' deference of expression and their care to win royal approval on sensitive issues, such as foreign policy or court and military appointments, does not alter the fact that in the last resort they held the whip hand. They might explain to George II (as to an obtuse pupil) that all they were doing was for his benefit, that without these necessary measures they could not get his business – in other words, supply – through the Commons [*Docs. 34; 35*]. They might have genuine reservations about the propriety of cajoling or bullying the king. In the last resort, however, they could get their way by mass resignation. In 1746 the Pelhams and their followers resigned because the king would not follow their advice. The king's favourites, Lords Granville and Bath, tried to form a ministry but could not carry the Commons. George had to take the Pelhams back on their own terms [102] [*Doc. 36*].

The Crown's effective power was not entirely destroyed. A king could still choose his ministers, but only from those enjoying the confidence of Parliament. George III was more determined than his grandfather and the fragmentation of political groups in the 1760s gave him (temporarily) a wider choice than usual. He made many suggestions on matters of detail but (as under George II) the broad lines of policy were laid down by his ministers, with his approval.

With the re-emergence of ideological divisions and of a popular dimension to politics, the king's personal authority dwindled further. He could still refuse to employ certain individuals or to approve certain policies (as with George III and Catholic emancipation), but he was no longer responsible for formulating policy. He was little more than a chairman of a committee, which asked his opinion for politeness' sake, but which reached major decisions without necessarily taking his views into account. When George III died, the monarch was well on the way to becoming a figurehead whose influence, such as it was, was mainly informal.

Because the monarch's personal power declined so much faster and so much more completely in practice than in theory, it is extremely difficult to chart the stages in its decline, but clearly the Revolution was of fundamental importance. Although the men of 1689 had not intended to deprive the king of effective power, they quite deliberately reserved to Parliament the financial leverage to ensure that his power would not be abused. On occasion (notably under William) the Commons as a whole felt sufficiently outraged to use that power to extort concessions from the king. Increasingly, however, it was the politicians who used their control of the Commons, a control strengthened by party ties, to force themselves and their followers into office and to force their policies on the monarch. They then used this control over patronage and policies to strengthen their control over the Commons. In the early Hanoverian period, the main beneficiaries of the Revolution seemed to be the Whig oligarchs who exploited the legacy of the Revolution to dominate both the Crown and Parliament [103]. Not until new popular political issues challenged the politicians' direction of policy and economic reform eroded their powers of patronage did the Commons begin to realise their potential, and Britain begin to move hesitantly towards parliamentary democracy.

11 THE LAW AND LOCAL GOVERNMENT

Both the Bill of Rights and the 'heads of grievances' sought to prevent any recurrence of the misuse of the legal system in the 1680s. Blatant interference with the processes of justice came to an end in 1689. Although before 1701 there was no law against the king's dismissing judges, William respected their independence. The Trials for Treason Act of 1696 removed some of the disadvantages of the accused: they were now allowed counsel and a copy of the indictment; they could challenge up to thirty-five of those named as jurors; above all, two witnesses were now required for a conviction. Together with the Habeas Corpus Act of 1679 (temporarily suspended in 1689–90), these measures did much to secure the liberty of the individual against the state. Political trials did not come to an end: the law was sometimes misused against Jacobite plotters and publishers, but not until the Jacobin trials of the 1790s were the courts again used systematically against political dissidents.

The liberalisation was not universal. The Riot Act of 1715 made it lawful for troops to fire on rioters (or demonstrators) who failed to disperse after due warning: hitherto, soldiers who shot rioters were liable to be indicted for murder. Moreover, if the law became more respectful of individual liberty, it also, in some respects, became more severe in its defence of property. Magistrates began to redefine as theft practices which had once been seen as workers' perquisites, such as gleaning odd grains of corn at harvest time. The game laws restricted hunting rights to men of a certain rank or wealth: many poorer men were not allowed to hunt even on their own property. The growing incidence of deer-poaching (in which the poachers often blackened their faces or wore masks) prompted the passing of the Black Act of 1723, which created some fifty new capital offences [123]. The number of offences carrying the death penalty increased from about fifty in 1689 to over two hundred in 1800. The theft of goods worth one shilling was felony, punishable by death.

The fact that the criminal law was apparently being used more ruthlessly to protect certain types of property has led some historians to see it as a means of social control and class oppression (and to see crime as a form of social protest). According to this view, the landed elite, lacking the physical power to coerce the people, used the law, with its mixture of brutality, theatre and carefully staged shows of mercy to instil a climate of fear and to create an illusion of impartial justice [65; 123].

There are problems with this viewpoint. For a start, it divides society into 'the gentry' and the rest (the 'plebs') [122]: social stratification was far more complex, with a growing range of 'middling sorts' [44; 54]. While the number of capital offences increased, the new ones were often created as a result of a temporary panic, or were slight elaborations of existing offences. Only a small – and dwindling – proportion of convicted felons was executed: an average of fewer than one a year in Bristol between 1741 and 1832. Although the army could be used against rioters, it seldom was.

More fundamentally, this view ignores the extent of popular participation in the enforcement of the criminal law. With no police force, the initiative to prosecute in most cases of theft or assault lay with the victim (or their kin). It was often a last resort, after attempts to secure restitution or reconciliation had failed. The magistrate's role was mainly to facilitate the prosecution, by ensuring that the accused appeared in court. There the case went before a grand jury, which decided if there was a case to answer, and a trial jury, which decided if the accused was guilty – and of what: many were acquitted or found guilty of a lesser offence. In most theft cases, both perpetrator and victim were relatively poor: the rich were better able to protect their property. To focus on the game laws and deer-poaching is to treat as typical one of the few types of crime which clearly set poor against rich.

Normally, the criminal law, like the rest of the legal system, offered a 'resource' through which one citizen could secure redress against another. Insofar as the law was used as a means of social control, those who used it covered a much broader social spectrum, and those who were controlled covered a much narrower one (and one defined as much in moral as in socio-economic terms) than the 'class-conflict' model would suggest. Throughout the seventeenth century, parish elites took the lead in punishing 'disorderly' behaviour [129]. This continued into the first half of the eighteenth century, as the 'better sort' of villagers paid the costs of prosecuting those accused of property offences and set up workhouses to discipline the poor [83]; the Societies for the Reformation of Manners, and some magistrates, also used the law, to punish tipplers, whores and others perceived as deviants [24; 48; 112; 113].

Even if one does not accept that the criminal law was used to maintain gentry hegemony, it is still possible to argue that the landed elite gained considerably from the Revolution. Secure from the threat of absolutism, the nobility and gentry continued to dominate politics and local government and were the main recipients of the government's increased patronage. They exploited their dominance of Parliament to pass laws protecting their property and to advance their economic interests, for example, through Enclosure and Turnpike Acts. Before the civil wars, governments had been concerned to keep grain prices down, by ensuring markets were supplied at reasonable prices and banning exports in time of dearth. From 1673, faced with falling grain prices, Parliament tried to keep prices up, by encouraging exports through a system of bounties. Whereas before the government had tried to help the poor partly by relief, through the poor laws, and partly by trying to keep grain affordable, by the end of the seventeenth century it relied mainly on the former.

This was not necessarily to the disadvantage of the poor. True, those regarded as undeserving could be denied relief or sent to the house of correction. The 1662 Act of Settlement made it easier for overseers of the poor or magistrates to exclude 'undesirables' from a parish. This led to many acts of petty tyranny – pregnant girls were shunted from one parish to another, as each tried to avoid the cost of raising the child. But the tyranny of overseers was often offset by the humanity of magistrates, who had a less direct interest in keeping down the poor rate of a particular parish. Moreover, the sums raised by the poor rate doubled or even trebled in the second half of the seventeenth century and continued to rise in the early eighteenth: one reason for setting up workhouses was the hope of reversing this trend.

In poor relief as in much else, the central government left local magistrates to their own devices: Parliamentary initiatives on local government seldom came from the Crown or its ministers. After 1689, apart from the occasional investigation of Papists, central government showed no interest in religious nonconformity. It expected JPs to ensure that taxes were collected and knew that it could rely on them to maintain law and order. It saw local offices primarily as political patronage and milked them of every drop of electoral advantage [58; 87]. After 1715, ministers also encouraged the creation of Whig oligarchies in the towns.

The governors of the shires and towns had the opportunity to use their power for their own selfish interests and many did so. Others discharged their duties conscientiously, as we have seen in relation to the poor law. For sound economic reasons, town corporations developed amenities – walks, assembly rooms, bowling greens – designed to make them attractive to the gentry and sought to improve the appearance of the houses on the major streets [30]. In many towns each citizen had traditionally been responsible for paving, cleaning and lighting the street outside his house. This proved impossible to enforce. As towns grew, their streets deteriorated and became more insanitary. Many corporations set up commissions (usually by Act of Parliament) to take over these functions and recouped the cost by means of a local rate.

In the shires, a constant stream of legislation extended the tasks (and cost) of local government. JPs took over responsibility from the parishes for the upkeep of major roads and bridges, raising the money by a county rate. The number of JPs grew and they supervised closely the selection, conduct and accounts of parish officials. The growing professionalism that we have seen in central government was also apparent in supposedly 'amateur' local government. Procedures became more elaborate and more uniform; printed forms were increasingly used; accounts were demanded more often from those handling public money; and systems of rewards and punishments were established. The demand for greater rigour and accountability came both from above – from Parliament and the JPs – and from the parishes – or at least from the 'better sort' there [83; 87]. The history of local government in the eighteenth century may not be glamorous, but there is more than enough evidence of public spirit and competence to disprove the claim that government was carried on by the rich for the benefit of the rich. While a lucky few gorged themselves on central government patronage, and others picked up scraps, many more participated, unpaid, in the government of county, town and parish out of a sense of civic duty, just as their forebears had done under the Tudors.

12 PARTIES AND THE WORKING OF POLITICS

One problem facing the historian of politics is that of motivation. How far are people concerned with power and profit and how far with issues of principle? If it is naive to see parliamentary debates as abstract discussions of political philosophy, it is usually over-cynical to dismiss them as a smokescreen of rhetoric behind which politicians pursued sordid material ambitions. There were times when political issues apparently counted for little, but this was not true of the generation after 1689. The nation was divided on important issues of principle, which complicated, and gave an added ferocity to, the perennial power-struggles of politicians, who combined strong ideological commitment with a large measure of greed and cynicism [Doc. 40].

Before considering the nature of party divisions, a brief functional analysis of the Commons would be helpful. By far the largest element consisted of 'backbenchers' – landowners, merchants, lawyers, army officers and minor officials. Such men had many reasons for entering Parliament, ranging from family tradition to a desire to make profitable business or professional contacts. Some were sturdily independent, others eagerly sought rewards for themselves and their families. The one thing they had in common was that they did not see themselves as candidates for major office: they lacked the time, the interest, the connections, the experience or the ability. The second group, much smaller, were the London-based career civil servants. Most were men of lukewarm (or non-existent) party loyalties, professionals for whom election to Parliament was part of the job. They spoke mainly on the affairs of their own departments and normally defended official policy. Thirdly, there were politicians, men who had or wanted major office, who pretended to some talent as administrators or debaters. In office, they usually defended ministerial policy. Out of office, they denounced the folly and corruption of the existing administration. Often, however, a ministry (especially a mixed ministry) was divided within itself. On such occasions it was common for ministers to attack their supposed colleagues [*Doc. 41*].

The politicians and civil servants provided most of the regular speakers in the Commons, but they could achieve little without backbench support. Even if their motives were factious and selfish, they had to couch their arguments in terms of principle and the public good. These arguments would have been ineffectual had not the principles to which they appealed been widely shared. With that in mind, let us consider the two axes along which men divided in this period – Court against Country and Whig against Tory.

These two divisions did not necessarily coincide. The Commons would not divide along the same lines on a 'Country' issue as they would on a 'party' issue. These were, moreover, different kinds of division. 'Court-Country' divisions centred on attitudes to the executive. The 'Court' in any division consisted of those siding with the king's ministers on that particular issue; the 'Country' of those against them. More fundamentally, the 'Country' expressed distrust of those in power. The approach of most 'Country' MPs was essentially negative. They did not want power themselves, but criticised the abuses of those who exercised it. Many were profoundly suspicious of the corrupt ways of the capital, of courtiers and civil servants. There was thus a certain nebulousness about 'Court-Country' divisions. If some criticised the king's ministers with sturdy consistency, others' attitudes varied, depending on who was in power and the issue in question. Traditional backbench ideals of independent MPs, making up their minds on each issue according to its merits, prevented 'Court-Country' divisions from attaining the rigidity and formality of a party system. Often a maverick 'Country' MP decided that this time the ministers were in the right or allowed personal obligations to a minister to change his mind. Often the pull of patronage or party loyalty outweighed the appeal of 'Country' principles [34; 63; 66; 67].

The division between Whig and Tory was different in kind. The core of the 'Court' comprised those in power for the time being. The 'Country' mostly did not want power. Whigs and Tories both sought power in order to implement their party programme [*Doc. 40*]. While it was not always possible to label an MP as 'Court' or 'Country' – many flitted from one to the other – it was easier to classify an individual as 'Whig' or 'Tory'. The surviving division lists show that most MPs supported one party consistently on the major issues which divided Whig from Tory, especially under Anne. Between 1690 and 1700 the predominant issues divided

'Court' and 'Country', with 'party' issues surfacing comparatively rarely. Under Anne the major issues were party issues and contemporaries could predict how MPs would vote with an accuracy that had not been possible in the 1690s. The rage of party permeated all aspects of English life. From Parliament and parliamentary elections, party feelings reached out into municipal politics and appointments to local office. There were Whig and Tory clubs, theatres, race-meetings, even doctors. The party identities thus created had a definition and a permanence never acquired by 'Court' and 'Country'. They also acquired an organisation, in the constituencies, in the political clubs and taverns of London and in both Houses of Parliament, where the Whigs built up an effective system of party whips and discipline [63; 70; 103; 116].

Whether 'Court-Country' or 'Whig-Tory' divisions predominated depended mainly on the nature of the major issues at the time. The Convention Parliament was mostly concerned with the legacy and animosities of the 1680s, so 'Whig-Tory' divisions predominated. The 1690s saw various new issues, which owed much to the war and the strains it imposed, and which mostly set 'Country' against 'Court'. First, MPs complained of the unprecedented – some said unwarranted and insupportable – burden of taxation. They claimed that much was wasted or embezzled and that the figures they were given were designed to mislead. Some reeled off statistics (their origin and accuracy alike uncertain) which purported to show that the government had plenty of money and that king and taxpayer were being cheated by the administration [*Doc. 37*]. Second, fears grew that the government's greater financial and patronage resources posed a real threat to Parliament's independence [*Doc. 38*]. The response was the Triennial Act and a series of bills designed to exclude placemen of various types from the Commons. The total exclusion of placemen in the Act of Settlement [*Doc. 31*] was unrealistic – it would have made it impossible for the House to receive any accurate information about finance or administration – and it was repealed before it could take effect. Certain categories of revenue officers were excluded, however, and others had to seek re-election after accepting office.

Linked to this question of the Crown's influence was the resentment of a largely landed parliament at the rise of the monied interest. Bankers and stockjobbers, it was believed, were less worthy of trust than landed men. In times of national peril, they could take their gold and flee. The landed men could not: their wealth was literally part of England. Many believed that landownership, over the generations, inculcated an integrity and public spirit not found in those whose wealth came from speculation and usury. To stop monied men buying their way into Parliament, an Act of 1710 (never fully enforced) laid down that county MPs should have a minimum income from land of £600 a year and borough MPs one of £300.

A third object of 'Country' anxiety was the standing army, which might enable the Crown to break through the restrictions on its power imposed since 1689 and to levy money at will. William had long been suspected, in Holland and in England, of absolutist ambitions. When peace was signed in 1697, he had an army on foot (most of it in Flanders) of about sixty thousand, similar in size to Cromwell's and three times as large as James II's. It was argued that standing armies were found only in absolutist states. England, surrounded by sea, had less need than most of such an army: the navy, backed by a citizen militia, should suffice [*Doc. 39*]. The 'Country' element in Parliament used the power of the purse to force William to cut the army to around six thousand.

A final feature of the 'Country' mentality was dislike of foreigners, at the heart of which lay a strong hostility to the Dutch. In 1689, the role of Dutch soldiers in conquering England was all too apparent and the Commons had to vote £600,000 for their services. Resentment of 'unfair' Dutch commercial competition remained strong. Many complained that vast sums were spent defending the Republic against the French, while the Dutch stole England's trade [68 chapter by Israel]. 'Dutch William' spent each summer abroad and made little effort to make himself agreeable to the English [*Doc. 16*]. At first he relied mainly on Dutchmen, Huguenots and Germans to command his armies, thinking them more experienced and trustworthy than the English. This annoyed the Commons. 'Englishmen naturally love their country and will not willingly destroy their country', declared one MP in 1692. 'Foreigners cannot have that affection for England' [7 vol. X p. 253]. The Commons demanded that in future only British-born subjects should be commissioned as officers. A similar chauvinism was apparent in the debates on William's Irish land grants. In 1699 the Commons resolved that all foreigners (except Anne's husband, Prince George) should be excluded from William's counsels and a similar provision was included in the Act of Settlement.

'Country' sentiment was not just an inchoate and negative expression of backbench anger. Attacks on mismanagement focused on individual ministers and were usually led by politicians, often their nominal colleagues: 'I believe what is done is rather designed against persons than to rectify things', remarked Seymour [15 *p. 295*]. In 1692 the Whig politicians Wharton and Montagu led a series of attacks on the Secretary of State, the Tory Earl of Nottingham. They accused him of mismanaging naval affairs and of disloyalty, on the grounds that he had opposed declaring the throne vacant and making William king in 1689 [*Doc. 41*]. One should not, however, conclude that 'Country' issues were raised only to promote personal or party ends, or that simple-minded backbenchers were constantly manipulated by unscrupulous politicians. 'Country' sentiment had a vitality and rationale of its own, which cut across party lines. If its main emphasis was negative, it was not always so, as was shown by the Commissions of Accounts of the 1690s.

From early in the reign Harley, Foley and others complained of the difficulty of obtaining reliable figures when assessing how much the Commons should vote. 'It concerns us to give the king a supply', said Foley in 1690, 'but it concerns us as much not to give more than is necessary. We have strange accounts of the revenue. I hope our case is not so bad as is represented; ... let us have a fair account' [7 vol. X *p. 28*]. William was quite willing to produce accounts, which would show how inadequate his revenue was. For this reason, some older 'Country' MPs were against it. 'I would enter upon accounts no further than to supply the present occasion', declared William Garroway in 1689. 'The deeper we entered on accounts, the deeper was always the charge. I have ever found it' [7 vol. IX *pp. 429–30*]. At the end of 1690, however, the Commons named the nine MPs who were to serve on the Commission of Accounts for the following year.

Most of the nine were Whigs, but the Commission included the staunch Tory, Sir Thomas Clarges, who joined with men of Whiggish origins like Foley and Harley in investigating financial mismanagement and in trying to overcome the obstruction and evasion of civil servants. If the Commission unearthed few major scandals, its very existence acted as a deterrent. Its reports enabled MPs to offer better-informed criticism of the Crown's financial demands and to prune the annual estimates for the armed forces. Its reports also served a constructive purpose. They helped mitigate the ignorance of many backbenchers about money matters and the true cost of the war. The Commission deserves some credit for the Commons' increasingly constructive approach to both taxation and borrowing during the 1690s [53; 54]. In 1692, the Commons complained about subsidies which William had promised to pay to Savoy and Hanover. Harley and Foley thereupon carried a proposal to include them under the general heading of 'hospitals, contingencies and extraordinary charges' [15].

The Commission of Accounts was a striking expression of a developing 'Country' mentality, which threatened, in the 1690s, to supersede the divisions of Whig and Tory. The Commission lapsed in 1697 after the exclusion in 1696 of three Tories who refused to subscribe the Association, which styled William 'rightful and lawful' king. The next year the Whig ministers sought to pack the Commission with their nominees, whereupon the Commons failed to renew it [74].

The possibility of creating a 'Country' party always depended on there being no strong 'Whig-Tory' issues to outweigh 'Country' loyalties. In 1700–2 the party issues of the 1680s again came to the fore, albeit in modified forms, and the chances of a new political alignment were doomed. Even so, the preponderance of 'Country' issues in the 1690s had one lasting effect on party divisions. Before 1689 Whigs had been suspicious of the Crown's power and influence – an essentially 'Country' outlook. Most Tories, too, were country gentlemen, suspicious of the corrupt ways of courtiers and civil servants, but fear of revolt and republicanism led them to magnify the Crown's authority. James's misconduct and William's usurpation forced them to rethink their position. Tories like Clarges opposed William's being made king and did their utmost to limit his powers. In this, they found they had much in common with old-style 'Country' Whigs like Foley who had little time for the younger Whigs of the 'Junto' – Somers, Wharton, Montagu – who were eager for office and not scrupulous about their methods. The co-operation of Tories and Country Whigs in the 1690s did not lead to the formation of a new Country party, but it ended with many erstwhile Whigs (like Harley) throwing in their lot with the Tories. From the Court-Country battles of the 1690s emerged an enlarged and revitalised Tory party, with a strong 'Country' mentality [55; 63; 103].

Such a transformation was possible only because the Whigs had always been a motley coalition, held together by insistence on exclusion of Catholics from the throne. When that was achieved in 1689, their original *raison d'être* disappeared, although the succession question re-emerged after the death of the Duke of Gloucester. However, during the battle over exclusion, the parties had developed opposed stances on other questions of principle, which survived the Revolution and were to some extent transformed by it. They were to determine the shape of politics in the Convention Parliament and in the reign of Anne.

The first major difference between the parties concerned the nature of monarchy. To the Tories, monarchy and its powers were divinely ordained and active resistance to the king was inadmissible. To the Whigs, it was a traditional institution whose powers could be limited, if that seemed essential for the common good. While usually avoiding a clear exposition of a right of resistance, Whigs generally assumed that the subject's duty of obedience was not unconditional and could be overridden by the right of self-preservation.

We have seen how the Tories were embarrassed by James's misrule and his replacement by William. They disliked what had happened, but could see no alternative: they certainly did not want James back. 'The utmost necessity', said one 'made me break my oath to king James' [7]. Most found it difficult to take an oath of allegiance to William and Mary, even though the oath omitted the usual reference to their being 'rightful and lawful' monarchs [*Doc. 42*]. Their scruples were exploited by the Whigs, who sought to appropriate the sole credit for the Revolution and to argue that only they were truly committed to William's regime and so worthy of trust [26 ch. 1]. They argued that anyone who had opposed declaring the throne vacant should not be on the Council and tried repeatedly to strengthen the oath of allegiance. The Assassination Plot of 1696 provided a pretext to call on office-holders to subscribe an Association to defend William's person (which included the phrase 'rightful and lawful'). Some Tories quit, but most gritted their teeth and subscribed the Association and, in 1701, an oath abjuring the Pretender.

Although many Tories allowed their enthusiasm for divine right and non-resistance one last fling under Anne, they were moving towards a new definition of non-resistance, in which obedience was due to established authority or to the monarch in Parliament rather than to the monarch alone [*Doc. 43*]. Meanwhile the Whigs, who had never been entirely happy about avowing the subjects' right of resistance, came under Anne, to appreciate that those most likely to resist established authority were the Jacobites. They too began to stress the subject's duty to obey the powers that be. After 1714 the Tories' attachment to divine right was moribund and Whig and Tory views on the nature of monarchy and the question of resistance largely converged [50; 85].

The differences between Whig and Tory attitudes to monarchy had originally focused on the succession. For Tories, God had established the hereditary succession and men could not alter it. To the Whigs, hereditary right should normally be respected, but could be overridden if the national interest required it. These rival views were evident in the debates on the change of ruler in 1689, after which the question remained dormant until Gloucester died in 1700. The Tories reluctantly agreed that the Electress of Hanover was the next heir, but found the prospect distasteful: her hereditary claim was far weaker than William's had been. The eyes of some Tories turned to James's son, the Old Pretender: although a Papist, he was also a Stuart. As the Hanoverian succession loomed nearer, more and more Tories indulged in the fantasy that the Pretender might abandon his Catholicism and so qualify for the throne. Such fantasies were eagerly exploited by the Whigs, who raised the succession question whenever they could, arguing that the Tories were Jacobites and that only the Whigs were truly loyal to the Protestant succession.

This was not true. As one Jacobite remarked bitterly in 1715, the Tories were 'never right hearty for the cause till they are mellow, as they call it, over a bottle or two . . . they do not care for venturing their carcases any further than the tavern' [11 *p. 37*]. If the Tories were emotionally drawn to the Stuarts, reason led the majority to accept the Hanoverian succession. As in 1688–9 and in 1701, forced to choose between the Protestant religion and the hereditary principle, the great majority of Tories chose the former. However, a few did opt for the Pretender and many others accepted the Hanoverians with such bad grace that for another generation Whig politicians were able to make political capital out of the claim that all Tories were Jacobites [55; 70; 97].

Another major difference between the parties, also dating back to the Exclusion Crisis, concerned the Church. The majority of Tories were High Churchmen and believed that religion and morality had been trampled underfoot since the Toleration Act. They raged against occasional conformity and tried to tack a clause against it to the supply bill in 1704. Over the next few years their rage increased, as the Junto proposed to admit Dissenters to the universities, to grant toleration to Dissenters in Ireland and to naturalise thousands of Calvinists from the Palatinate. The last straw was the Whigs' impeachment of Dr Henry Sacheverell, a parson whose prejudices against Whiggery made up in vehemence what they lacked in coherence. He was impeached for a sermon in which he denied that resistance had occurred in 1688–9, but his prosecution was seen as yet another example of the Whigs' vindictiveness against the Church. In London a High Church mob smashed Dissenting meeting houses and the homes of leading Whigs; it was stopped by troops on its way to attack the Bank [72]. Sacheverell was convicted, but the Tories won the propaganda battle and the Lords imposed only a light punishment. The trial showed clearly the great strength of High Church sentiment and the unpopularity of Dissent.

The last major party issue was foreign policy. In the wars of 1689–97 and 1702–13, the Whigs argued that the French could be defeated only by a land campaign and that it was vital for England that Louis XIV should not overrun the Low Countries. The Tories claimed that land wars were unnecessary and expensive, that they benefited England's continental allies far more than England, and that national interests could best be served by a war against France's trade and colonies [*Doc. 44*]. The war of the Spanish succession was initially popular, thanks to Marlborough's victories, but later disillusionment set in. War taxation was high, casualties were heavy and the harvest of 1709 was the worst for many years. In these circumstances, many could not understand the Whigs' refusal to negotiate with Louis (who was offering generous terms) until such time as his grandson had been expelled from Spain, particularly as the Spaniards did not want him to go and the allies lacked the military resources to drive him out. The Tories won much popular support for their attack on the war and for their argument that it had become a device whereby the monied interest grew rich on the taxes paid by landowners and consumers [*Doc. 27*].

The popularity of the Tories' stand on the Church and foreign policy was demonstrated by their crushing victories in the general elections of 1710 and 1713, which did much to substantiate their claim to be the natural majority party. To Bolingbroke, the Tories represented the true English interest while the Whigs represented sectional and often alien interests: England's foreign allies, the monied men, the Dissenters [*Doc. 40*]. Election results tended to bear out his claim. Elections under the Triennial Act were freer and more frequent than ever before: ten between 1695 and 1715. (Charles II's reign saw only four general elections, three of them in 1679–81.) Neither William nor Anne interfered systematically in elections, because to do so would provoke criticism and because they wished neither party to win a crushing victory. The electorate grew larger (in percentage terms) than it was to be *after* the Great Reform Bill of 1832. Inflation reduced the value of property qualifications for voting, especially in the counties. In many boroughs the uncertainties of the franchise were exploited by whichever party stood to gain from an enlarged electorate. In many constituencies the electorate grew too large to be bribed or browbeaten and had to be wooed by the two parties, but even in small boroughs, rival contestants could give voters a choice. Electors were influenced as much as the ruling elite by the issues of the day. Most constituencies had two members and the great majority of electors voted for two Whig or two Tory candidates, rather than one of each. Electors also changed their minds according to the issues of the moment: the large and independent electorate of London, for instance, voted in four Whigs in 1708 and four Tories in 1710 [71; 103; 116].

Under Anne the Tories were usually more successful than the Whigs in appealing to the electors. Only in 1708 did the Whigs win a clear victory; they were humiliated in 1710 and 1713. The Tories' great assets were resentment of war taxation and commitment to the Church, of which only the second remained important throughout the reign. It is hard now to think of the Church of England as militant, but it had massive popular support under Anne and its clergy ruthlessly attacked Dissenters and Whigs. On the eve of the Sacheverell riots, one London parson preached on the text: 'Break their teeth, O God, in their mouths.' The Tories exploited a growing hostility to Dissent, a hostility all the greater when those Dissenters were immigrants, like the 'poor Palatines'.

Against this all the Whigs had to offer was anti-Popery and the claim that the Tories were Jacobites. Their victory in 1708 followed an attempted Jacobite rising in Scotland and their triumph in 1715 owed much to the fear that the Tories wished to bring in the Pretender. The Whigs gained a virtual monopoly of George I's favour, but could not trust the electors to vote them in again. They began to extend techniques which they had already begun to use, designed to ensure a constant Whig majority in the Commons. Whig magnates like the Dukes of Newcastle and Devonshire enlarged their empires of pocket boroughs. Every scrap of local patronage was used to the Whigs' electoral advantage. Political considerations governed the appointment of customs and excise men, of army officers in garrison towns, of bishops and canons in cathedral cities. The Commons Committee of Elections and Privileges showed (as always) a strong party bias in deciding election disputes. Above all, the Septennial Act of 1716 ensured that MPs had to face the electors only every seven years rather than every three. As a result, election results ceased to reflect swings of public opinion. Despite the Excise Crisis of 1733, Walpole's majority was almost unchanged in 1734. The Tories continued to do well in the counties and the more open boroughs, but the Whigs controlled enough of the small boroughs (and the forty-five Scottish MPs who sat at Westminster after the Union) to ensure an unassailable majority. In many constituencies, Tories ceased to stand as they had no chance of winning: some even defected to the Whigs. Contests became rarer. Only in a minority of constituencies was the electoral vigour of Anne's reign sustained [42; 71; 89; 103].

It is one of history's many ironies that so soon after the Revolution provoked (in part) by James II's attempts to pack Parliament, the electoral system should have been perverted, more subtly but more effectively, by Walpole. The Bill of Rights' ringing declaration 'that election of Members of Parliament ought to be free' must have sounded hollow in the 1730s. By then, the energy and the willingness to innovate which were so apparent in the 1690s had become overlaid by conservatism and complacency. The Whig party, which had once stood for 'clean' government and religious liberty, now raised political 'corruption' to a level of unparalleled sophistication and quietly forgot the interests of the Dissenters [85]. Both old-fashioned radical Whigs and maverick Tories like Bolingbroke denounced Walpole for betraying 'Revolution principles' and wondered if they were really any better off as a result of the Revolution: the corrupting influence of money seemed to rule all.

Such jeremiads were unduly pessimistic. Walpole depended as much on pursuing policies acceptable to backbench MPs as on the use of patronage. If he and the Pelhams met with so little opposition, this was, in part, a tribute to their understanding of the moods and prejudices of the Commons, which enabled them to avoid contentious issues, and to their willingness to back down if by chance such issues arose. (This was the case with both the excise scheme and the Jew bill of 1753.) Such an approach was made easier by the demise of the great issues of Anne's reign. The great majority of Tories accepted George I's accession and in time lost their sentimental fondness for the Stuarts. A long period of peace laid to rest the animosities aroused by the war of 1702–13. Even the Church ceased to be an issue: the Whig leaders of the later 1710s abandoned their predecessors' habit of baiting the Churchmen.

If the Commons temporarily became less responsive to the electorate, the Crown was becoming more dependent on those who could manage the Commons. When the electors' influence over the Commons' composition was restored in the nineteenth century, it was to prove far easier to force the people's wishes on the monarch than had been the case in the seventeenth. If the likes of Montesquieu and Voltaire exaggerated the liberty enjoyed by Englishmen and the merits of the British constitution, their writings are a salutary correction to Bolingbroke's pessimism and a reminder that, by continental standards, England was a free country with a liberal political system. It had solved by consent the problem of mobilising the nation's resources for war, a problem the French Crown had failed to solve by compulsion. Galling though it was for the French, England managed to combine its eccentric constitution with a power in world affairs out of all proportion to its size.

There is no indication that the men of 1688–9 had planned this. Their main aim had been self-preservation against the threat of 'Popery and arbitrary government'. Few had any conception of the feasibility of progress or of constitution-building. Most were suspicious of change and agreed to alter the constitution only when it seemed necessary to prevent other, more drastic, changes. The changes of 1688–9 were limited, unco-ordinated and pragmatic. They were not given coherence by the sort of ruthless logic which underlay France's administrative restructuring in the 1790s or the Code Napoléon.

And yet they worked. They left intact those elements of the medieval constitution (Parliament and a participatory system of local government and law enforcement) that preserved traditions of reciprocity and consent which, in many countries, were crushed with the advent of absolutism. Whereas the rigidity of absolutism could often be overcome only by violence, the flexibility of the British constitution allowed it to adapt to changing expectations and to the perception of new needs. If such a constitution, with all its surviving anomalies, smacks more of pragmatism than of logic, that in itself could be seen as typically English. This pragmatism, this preference for adapting the old rather than sweeping all away and starting afresh, was a feature of the Glorious Revolution. If we ask why England never underwent a revolution comparable with the French and Russian Revolutions, perhaps we should conclude, as Macaulay did, that one major reason was that England had undergone a bloodless revolution at the end of the seventeenth century [90].

13 SCOTLAND AND IRELAND

If the Revolution in England was bloodless, the same could not be said of Scotland or Ireland. The resistance of the Scottish Jacobites effectively ended in August 1689, at Dunkeld, but the war in Ireland dragged on for three years. There were a number of bloody battles – notably the Boyne and Aughrim – and a series of debilitating sieges, in which besiegers and besieged suffered heavy casualties. The armies of both sides plundered and rustled cattle more or less indiscriminately – one commander was said to have 'robbed the whole country about Mullingar as bad as the Turks can do at Belgrade' [137] – while the general disorder offered ample scope for freelance brigands – tories or rapparees. Even after formal hostilities ceased in 1691, brigandage remained endemic and the economic damage done by the wars took years to make good.

Quite apart from the human cost of the wars, the Revolution was also, in time, to transform the relationships of Scotland and Ireland with England. The three kingdoms had little in common under the Stuarts other than having the same king (and, for much of the population, the same language). In this the Stuart kingdoms resembled the 'composite monarchies' of continental Europe, agglomerations of territory brought together by dynastic accident (Scotland) or conquest (Ireland). Before Scotland's king inherited the English throne in 1603, the two nations' history had been characterised by mutual hostility. The Scots had their own Parliament, their own laws and their own Church, which was organised on Presbyterian lines. James I and Charles I tried to establish greater congruence between the Churches of the two kingdoms, but whereas James succeeded in reintroducing a measure of episcopacy, Charles provoked a nationwide revolt and the Scots unilaterally abolished bishops. Charles II re-established episcopacy, as a means of strengthening his control over the kingdom, but otherwise was wary of provoking the Scots and sought to keep Scotland quiet [32; 36].

Ireland had been conquered centuries before, but English rule normally sat lightly on most of the Irish, until the Reformation. The bulk of the population – not only the native Irish, but many members of the settler elite (the Old English) – remained obstinately Catholic. This created a serious problem of allegiance: if the pope declared an English monarch deposed (as he did Elizabeth in 1570) would the Irish rise up in revolt? Moreover, at a time when England was menaced by Spain, Ireland offered an obvious backdoor into England. Both these arguments were used by aggressive and acquisitive Englishmen, who insisted that Ireland must be subjugated and anglicised in the interests of English security and the advancement of Protestantism; the conquerors could also expect to profit handsomely from dispossessing the Catholics, Irish and Old English alike. After a long bitter revolt against the Dublin government at the end of Elizabeth's reign, James I began a policy of confiscation (of Catholics' lands) and plantation (of settlers from the mainland: mainly Scots in Ulster, mainly English elsewhere). English law increasingly superseded Irish law and Catholics were excluded from positions of power.

It might seem that these policies would provoke a movement for independence. In fact, the Catholics remained loyal to the monarch except when one section threw off their allegiance in the exceptional circumstances of civil war. Faced with the hostility of a growing Protestant (or New English) population, and a hostile English Parliament, the Catholics' best hope seemed to lie with the king, who was noticeably less anti-Catholic. The rebellion of 1641, which was to provide the pretext for the Cromwellian confiscations, was a response to the threat to the Catholics from the English Parliament and the Scots. Between 1640 and 1660, the Catholics' share of the land fell from around 60 per cent to under 20 per cent. Under Charles II, they mostly remained quiescent, fearful of provoking further punishment. Charles II's chief governor, the Duke of Ormond, saw the Ulster Scots as more of a threat than the Catholics [32; 98].

In recent years, historians have stressed the interaction of the Stuarts' three kingdoms, and indeed it is impossible to understand the outbreak of the civil war purely in English terms. That said, the extent of that interaction varied. There were some continual sources of friction (such as the links between the Ulster Scots and the radical Presbyterians of south-west Scotland) and English politicians watched warily for extensions of royal authority in Scotland or Ireland which might be replicated in England. However, Charles II was concerned mainly to keep his other two kingdoms quiet, although he did see Ireland as a supplementary source of revenue and, if need arose, soldiers. He avoided provoking the sort of resistance in Scotland or Ireland which had destabilised his father's composite monarchy from 1637. By contrast James II's open favour to Catholics in Ireland raised fears of Papist armies being brought over to subjugate the English and Scots. Once expelled from England, Ireland offered James a natural base from which to recover his Crowns, but he was far more concerned to regain England than he was to uphold the interests of the Catholics of Ireland [95; 114].

Scotland's Protestants, whether Episcopalian or Presbyterian, had been outraged by James VII and II's attempts to advance the interests of the nation's tiny Catholic minority. Although they played an even less active role than the English in James's expulsion, all factions sought to profit from his departure by securing rewards for themselves and the redress of grievances. As in England, in seeking William's favour those who might be labelled 'Whigs' had the advantage that they had no qualms about renouncing their allegiance to James; when the Jacobites rose in arms on James's behalf, their opponents denounced all Tories or episcopalians as a danger to the new regime. The Whigs' position was further strengthened by the fact that William knew little of Scottish affairs, while his preoccupations elsewhere – with unrest in the English army, the threat from Ireland and the continental war – made him eager to secure a settlement in Scotland as quickly as possible, even on terms that were less than advantageous.

William called a Convention at Edinburgh in March 1689. The withdrawal of James's supporters gave the Whigs a freer hand than their English counterparts and their Claim of Right, though based on the English Declaration of Rights, was far more radical. It declared that James had forfeited the throne by misgovernment, not just abdicated, called for the abolition of episcopacy and implied that the Crown was offered to William in the expectation that he would respect the nation's laws and liberties and that he would agree to measures brought in by Parliament to secure them [*Doc. 45*]. The wording was sufficiently ambiguous for William to deny that implication, but he found himself beset by demands to debar servants of the previous monarchs from office and to abolish the Lords of the Articles – a committee that included the king's leading ministers, who decided which bills were to be brought before Parliament [36; 78 Ch. 4].

As the 1689 Parliament failed to vote any revenue, William tried a more conciliatory approach in 1690, agreeing to the establishment of Presbyterianism and the abolition of the Articles. The former proved deeply divisive, as hardline Presbyterians rushed to drive out those clergy they regarded as episcopalian, often with the use of mob violence. Despite the Presbyterians' claim that the majority of the population was on their side, there was much support for episcopacy, especially in the north-east, and not all Presbyterians found the newly established brand of Presbyterianism congenial. The abolition of the Articles further hampered William's agents as they attempted to manage Parliament. Several rival magnates, each with blocs of followers among the burgh members, jockeyed for power, seeking to be bought off and refusing to co-operate with one another in pursuing the king's business. Scotland might have accepted William as king, but in many respects it was almost as independent of the Crown as it had been in the 1640s. A series of issues – notably English opposition to a Scottish settlement at Darien, in Panama – ensured that the Scots Parliament sustained a sense of grievance.

The problems raised by this lack of control over Scotland were increased by the death of the Duke of Gloucester. The Claim of Right recognised Anne as William's heir, but the Scots pointedly failed to follow England's example in the Act of Settlement and vest the succession in the House of Hanover. With Louis XIV recognising James III (and VIII), the Scots may well have believed that by keeping the succession open they enhanced their bargaining position: indeed, in 1703 an Act effectively excluded Hanover unless Scotland's government was freed of 'English or any foreign influence'. Another Act declared that the Scots Parliament – not the Crown – should decide on matters of peace and war, thus stripping the monarch of control of foreign policy. These provocative moves fuelled a growing conviction in England that Scotland must be brought to heel by an 'incorporating union', whereby Scotland's troublesome Parliament would be subsumed in a British Parliament, where the Scots would be comfortably outnumbered. For the English Tories, a union offered the added benefit of enabling them to aid the beleaguered Scottish episcopalians.

By 1704 the London government had accepted the need for union: the problem now was to sell the idea to the Scots. Three major inducements were used. First, the English Parliament responded to the threats in the Acts of 1703 by passing the Aliens Act: unless the Scots started negotiating for union within nine months, all estates in England owned by Scots would be forfeited and most imports from

Scotland would be banned. Second, the Scots were assured that they would retain their own law and Church. Third, they were to be allowed to trade freely throughout England's colonial empire: they had hitherto been excluded by the Navigation Acts. Beyond all this, Scottish politicians would gain access to the rich patronage of the London government and there were many allegations of bribery, and promises of gifts, to the commissioners who negotiated the union. This mixture of carrot and stick had its effect. The Treaty of Union of 1707 stipulated that Scotland should return forty-five MPs and sixteen representative peers to Westminster, which would henceforth legislate for Scotland; the Edinburgh Parliament ceased to exist [36; 69 Ch. 8, 106].

As the recent growth of Scottish nationalism has focused attention on Scotland's relationship with England, the question of the Act of Union has become politically charged. Historians of a nationalist persuasion tend to see it as the product of bribery and/or *force majeure*. A substantial element of both was present, but it is worth remarking that bribery had signally failed to bring the Scots Parliament to heel between 1689 and 1705. Moreover, while the threat of installing the Old Pretender as King of Scotland might be a useful weapon to use against the London government, it is unlikely that many leading Scottish politicians would have been prepared to carry it out: a Stuart might be welcome, a Catholic far less so. It is clear that there was much support for union in Scotland, especially among the merchants, and that, economically at least, Scotland benefited from it [127]. Ambitious Scots – writers and architects as well as politicians – found more scope for their talents, while culturally and educationally Scotland thrived. Much criticism of the union, in fact, came with hindsight as Scots realised that they had been subsumed into a much larger entity which showed little concern for Scottish interests and did not always adhere to the terms of the treaty. Expecting to be treated as full and equal citizens of 'Britain', they found that many of the English continued to regard them as inferior. Perhaps Scotland's greatest loss, with the union, was a sense of identity.

Whereas James II's policies found little support in England or Scotland, they were enthusiastically endorsed by the Catholic majority in Ireland. James was reluctant to proceed too vigorously, for fear of the possible reaction in England, which was always his main priority, and he was determined to maintain Ireland's subordination to England. His reluctance was gradually worn down by Richard Talbot, Earl of Tyrconnell, who displaced Clarendon as

Lord Deputy. Tyrconnell insisted that all the Protestants of Ireland were disaffected and only the Catholics were loyal. He replaced Protestants with Catholics in offices of all kinds, civilian and military, and disarmed the militia, through which the Protestants might have defended themselves. By the end of 1688 the army was predominantly Catholic and much of Ireland's government was in Catholic hands [95; 114].

When James fled from England, Tyrconnell (after some hesitation) set out to complete his control over Ireland, in the expectation of aid from France. He rapidly enlarged the army, gradually mopping up Protestant resistance; many Protestants fled to England, where possible taking their money with them. Soon the only Protestant strongholds were Londonderry and Enniskillen. The Jacobites failed to take either, even after James arrived with arms, money and military advisers from France, partly because of the tenacity of the defenders of Derry, partly because the Jacobites, although enthusiastic, were poorly organised and desperately short of serviceable weapons. With trade dead and agriculture badly disrupted, they were also short of money, which led them to issue new brass coins – even melting down brass cannon in order to do so.

While the siege of Derry dragged on, James called a Parliament in Dublin, which highlighted the differences between his policies and those of his followers. They wanted a reversal of a century of expropriation, passing a massive Act of Attainder to confiscate the estates of hundreds of Protestants. They also wanted to weaken England's power over Ireland: James reluctantly agreed to an Act stating that the English Parliament could not legislate for Ireland, but blocked a bill to repeal Poynings' Law (by which all bills for the Irish Parliament had to be approved by the English privy council) and the Navigation Acts (which subordinated Ireland's economic interests to England's). Nevertheless, he needed the Irish and they needed him. The failure to take Derry destroyed any prospect of a quick invasion of mainland Britain, but the army sent from England later in 1689 achieved little and was decimated by disease over the winter.

This served to convince William that he had to go to Ireland in person to end what he saw as an irritating distraction from the main theatre of war on the continent. His intervention seemed decisive: on 1 July 1690 he defeated the Jacobites at the crossing of the Boyne and marched on to Dublin, while James fled the country. But the Jacobites were not defeated and the war dragged on into 1691. William, frustrated, became desperate to end the war on more or less any terms [95; 96; 114]. As his forces besieged Limerick for the second time, agreement was finally reached. Under the treaty, all members of the Jacobite army were to be free to go abroad, with their arms and valuables. The clauses which related to the position of those Catholics who remained in Ireland were complex, but one was to cause particular controversy:

> The Roman Catholics of this kingdom shall enjoy such privileges in their exercise of their religion as are consistent with the laws of Ireland, or as they did enjoy in the reign of King Charles II; and their Majesties, as soon as their affairs will permit them to summon a Parliament in that kingdom, will endeavour to procure the said Roman Catholics such farther security in that particular as may preserve them from any disturbance on account of their said religion [2 p. 765].

William's eagerness to extricate himself from the war helps explain these concessions. He probably had considerable reservations about allowing the soldiers ('Wild Geese') to leave; transported at English expense, many thousands served in Louis XIV's armies (although their departure removed much of the remaining Jacobite military threat). But William probably had few qualms about conceding a measure of toleration to Catholics. Catholics enjoyed freedom of worship in the Dutch Republic and William was personally tolerant, had important Catholic allies (Spain, the Emperor) and had hoped to secure toleration for the English Catholics in 1689 [78 Ch. 3].

The Protestants of Ireland greeted the treaty with howls of rage. There had been many acts of violence by Catholics against Protestants during the wars, duly inflated by rumour and the press. These (in Protestant eyes) fell into a well-worn pattern of implacable Catholic savagery towards Protestants, as seen in the massacres of 1641 and the blanket condemnation of Protestants (to death and expropriation) in the Attainder Act of 1689. Both a lust for revenge and a concern for self-preservation militated against any concessions to Papists. The land clauses of the Treaty were interpreted in such a way as to declare forfeit as many Catholics' estates as possible, while successive Irish Parliaments, far from confirming the religious provisions of the treaty, enacted new penal laws against the Catholics [114].

James II's reign and the Jacobite wars represented the last chance for the Catholics of Ireland to reverse a century of expropriation and exclusion from power. Not all Catholics lost their land in the forfeitures that followed the wars, but the small surviving band of Catholic landowners gradually withered away. Some families died out, some Catholics converted in order to qualify for office. A new Act laid down that Catholics had to divide their land equally between their sons – but if one son turned Protestant, it would all go to him. While there was little consistent persecution, Catholics were in most respects second-class citizens. For the moment, while there was much surly resentment and some agrarian violence, there was little concerted resistance to Protestant rule. The days of Catholic nationalism lay in the future.

For the Protestants, on the face of it, life was good – at least for those enjoying full political rights, from which Dissenters, including the Ulster Presbyterians, were excluded. Dublin enjoyed an unprecedented prosperity and elegance in the eighteenth century as the Anglo-Irish elite, like their English counterparts, enjoyed the fruits of government patronage. Their ability to do so, however, was built upon a number of unresolved tensions, at the root of which lay the ambiguities of 'Anglo-Irish' identity [22; 26 Ch. 4]. On one hand, they thought of themselves as English, bringing English civility and civilisation to a barbarous land; on the other, as generation succeeded generation, they became increasingly rooted in Ireland and increasingly aware of clashes between English and Irish interests. The English view of the Anglo-Irish was equally ambivalent: they were, like the American colonists, seen as English – kith and kin – in some respects, but also as having forfeited their birthright as true Englishmen by leaving England. These tensions were most apparent over questions of economic interest. The English believed that colonies existed for the benefit of the mother country, the colonists (including the Anglo-Irish) deeply resented the sacrificing of colonial interests for English profit: thus the English Parliament forbade imports of Irish cattle into England and did its utmost to kill off Ireland's woollen industry, to prevent it from competing with England's.

Clashes of economic interest led to the wider question of how far the English Parliament could legislate for Ireland. (There had never been any suggestion that it could legislate for Scotland.) The Irish argued that the Dublin Parliament was as sovereign within Ireland as the Westminster Parliament was within England: bills might (under Poynings' Law) have to be approved by the English privy council before they could be brought in, but it was the Irish Parliament that gave them legal force. On a number of occasions during the Jacobite wars the English Parliament debated bills relating to Ireland. As the dispute heated up in the late 1690s, the English Parliament asserted, in an address to the king, that it could legislate for Ireland [2].

This is not to suggest that the Anglo-Irish sought independence from England: quite the contrary. Some called for a union, to bring to an end Ireland's colonial status. More fundamentally, however much they might extol the achievements of the men of Derry and Enniskillen in 1689, they were only too aware that Protestant rule in Ireland had been saved by English military intervention and that its continuance depended on England. Conversely, the English needed the Protestants to police the Catholic majority: so long as the French wars continued, the risk remained that the Catholics might revolt and offer Louis a base from which to attack England.

The relationship between the English government and the Anglo-Irish was not an easy one. The issues of trade and English claims of a right to legislate for Ireland – together with friction over the Treaty of Limerick and land forfeitures – ensured that managing the Irish Parliament in the 1690s was difficult. Successive viceroys tried not to offend Anglo-Irish sensibilities, rewarded compliant or influential MPs and asked for little in taxation: Ireland (like Scotland [36]) underwent no 'financial revolution' in the 1690s and, compared with England, both were lightly taxed. This preferential treatment continued in the eighteenth century. Anglo-Irish 'undertakers', dispensing generous patronage, ensured the smooth running of each session; the occasional gaffe from London was followed by a further shower of rewards (including a brand new Parliament House). Thus, while the Scots were uncomfortably subsumed into 'Great Britain', the Anglo-Irish minority continued to enjoy a considerable measure of *de facto* autonomy. When the agitations in America provoked echoes in Ireland, Westminster at last formally conceded that it could not legislate for Ireland. Only with the rise of nationalism in the wake of the French Revolution did this cosy relationship come to an end. Then, and only then, were Irish politics dominated once more by questions of Catholic against Protestant, Irish against English, and the struggle for supremacy which seemed to have been resolved in 1689–91 broke out anew.

PART FOUR: DOCUMENTS

DOCUMENT 1   ANTI-POPERY

This typical Exclusionist pamphlet describes the horrors which would allegedly ensue if England had a Catholic ruler.

First, imagine you see the whole town in a flame, occasioned this second time by the same Popish malice which set it on fire before. At the same instant, fancy that amongst the distracted crowd you behold troops of Papists ravishing your wives and daughters, dashing your little children's brains out against the walls, plundering your houses and cutting your own throats by the name of heretic dogs. Then represent to yourselves the Tower playing off its cannon and battering down your houses about your ears. Also, casting your eye towards Smithfield, imagine you see your father, or your mother, or some of your nearest and dearest relations, tied to a stake in the midst of flames, when with hands and eyes lifted up to heaven they scream and cry out to that God for whose cause they die, which was a frequent spectacle the last time Popery reigned amongst us. ... Your trading's bad, and in a manner lost already, but then the only commodity will be fire and sword, the only object women running with their hair about their ears, men covered with blood, children sprawling under horses' feet and only the walls of houses left standing ...

C. Blount, 'An Appeal from the Country to the City' (1679), reprinted in *State Tracts*, 2 vols, London, 1689–92, vol. I, pp. 401–2.

DOCUMENT 2   JAMES II'S POLITICAL CREED

Unlike James I, James II was no philosopher, but while in exile he drew up some papers of advice for his son, which give an insight into his views on kingship.

Kings being accountable for none of their actions but to God and themselves ought to be more cautious and circumspect than those who are in lower stations and as 'tis the duty of subjects to pay true allegiance to him and to observe his laws, so a king is bound by his office to have a fatherly love and care of them. ... Consider you come into the world to serve God Almighty and not only to please yourself and that by Him kings reign and that without His particular protection nothing you undertake can prosper. ... Therefore preserve your prerogative, but disturb not the subjects in their property nor conscience, remember the great precept, Do as you would be done to, for that is the law and the prophets ...

J. S. Clarke (ed.), *Life of James II*, 2 vols, London, 1816, vol. II, pp. 619–21.

DOCUMENT 3   **JAMES AND THE SUCCESSION**

Although many feared that James planned to change the succession in favour of a Catholic, this letter (written to a leading Catholic extremist, who supported such a change) shows that he had no such intention.

Not only could it never enter my head to think of changing it, but I know well that it is not in my power to do it, even if a Pope and a Parliament joined with me. For where the crown is hereditary (as it is in these kingdoms, thanks be to God) His Almighty power alone can dispose of it, not only the hearts of kings but their crowns being in His hands ...

James to Albeville, c. 29 March 1687, Archives des Affaires Etrangères, Paris, Correspondance Politique, Angleterre 164, fol. 28.

DOCUMENT 4   **JAMES'S REASONS FOR BECOMING A CATHOLIC**

In 1687 James wrote to his daughter Mary, urging her to follow his example and become a Catholic.

Surely it is only reasonable that this Church, which has a constant succession from the time of the apostles to the present, should be more in the right than those private men who, under the pretext of reformation, have been the authors of new opinions. ... It was this consideration which principally led me to embrace the communion of the Roman Church, there being no other which claims, or can claim, infallibility, for there must necessarily be an infallible Church, or otherwise what Our Saviour said cannot be and the gates of Hell would prevail against her ...

M. Bentinck (ed.), *Lettres et Mémoires de Marie, Reine d'Angleterre*, The Hague, 1880, pp. 7–8.

DOCUMENT 5   THE FRENCH AMBASSADOR'S VIEW OF
JAMES'S INTENTIONS

*Barrillon knew James very well and naturally did not share his subjects' fear
and hatred of Catholicism and absolutism. He was quite sure that James's
main aim was to promote his religion.*

As far as I can see, the King is sincerely concerned to leave (the Catholics)
in security after his death, because the ardour with which he seeks the
repeal of the penal laws is more for their sake than his own, and although
he often says, when talking of the revocation of the Test oath, that he
would risk everything rather than allow his subjects to take an oath by
which they declare him an idolater, it is also a question of the security of
the Catholics, whose lives and safety will be at the mercy of his successor
and of Parliament if these laws are still in being on the day of his death.

Barrillon to Louis XIV, 11/21 July 1687, Public Record Office, PRO
31/3/171.

DOCUMENT 6   GODDEN V. HALES

*This test case was designed to secure a ruling from the judges upholding the
dispensing power.*

We think we may very well declare the opinion of the court to be that the
king may dispense in this case; and the judges go upon these grounds:

1. That the kings of England are sovereign princes.
2. That the laws of England are the king's laws.
3. That therefore 'tis an inseparable prerogative in the kings of England
   to dispense with penal laws in particular cases and upon particular
   necessary reasons.
4. That of those reasons and those necessities the king himself is sole
   judge ...
5. This is not a trust ... granted to the king by the people, but the
   ancient remains of the sovereign power and prerogative of the kings
   of England, which never yet was taken from them, nor can be.

Kenyon, [13], p. 404.

DOCUMENT 7   THE DISPENSING POWER CONDEMNED

In the trial of the Seven Bishops, Mr Justice Powell made it clear that he thought James's use of the dispensing power had gone far beyond what the judges had considered acceptable in 1686.

Gentlemen, we must consider what they [the bishops] say is illegal in it. They say, they apprehend the declaration is illegal because it is founded upon a dispensing power which the king claims, to dispense with the laws concerning ecclesiastical affairs. Gentlemen, I do not remember any case in all our law ... that there is any such power in the king and the case must turn upon that ... I can see no difference, nor know of one in law, between the king's power to dispense with laws ecclesiastical and his power to dispense with any other laws whatsoever. If this be once allowed of, there will need no Parliament; all the legislature will be in the king, which is a thing worth considering and I leave the issue to God and your consciences.

Kenyon, [13], p. 410.

DOCUMENT 8   INSTRUCTIONS TO ELECTION AGENTS, 1688

The agents, many of them former Exclusionists, had two tasks: to provide the central government with detailed information about local politics and personalities and to influence as many electors as possible in favour of repealing the penal laws and Test Acts.

1. You shall make the king's declaration [of indulgence] the chief subject of your discourse with such persons as you shall think fit to speak with. ...

6. You are to make acquaintance with the leading, active and interested men in the county, or in the towns and corporations, who are inclinable to abrogate the penal laws for religion and the tests, and engage them to improve their interest for effecting it.

7. You are to inform yourself (as privately as may be) whether the persons proposed to be chosen, by the list given you, be right-principled and so disposed to part with the laws as may be depended on.

8. You are to inform yourself whether the regulations made in the respective corporations have been of proper persons for His Majesty's service.

9. You are to inform yourself who are the electors in the respective corporations and boroughs, and by what manner elections are made, who influences them, and who are fittest to be chosen in those places where none are yet proposed.

10. You are to inform yourself of the behaviour of the officers of the several branches of His Majesty's revenue in relation to elections, whether they promote His Majesty's interest as they ought to do ...

11. [You are] to acquaint yourselves with the preachers of the Dissenting congregations and to encourage them to employ their interest for the abrogating those laws and tests. ...

12. You are to inform yourself of some fit person in each corporation with whom a correspondence may be held for the knowledge of the true state of the same, and to whom books and pamphlets may be sent, to disperse them for the people's better information ...

J. P. Kenyon, *The Stuart Constitution*, 1st edn, Cambridge, 1966, pp. 509–10.

DOCUMENT 9   AN ELECTION AGENT AT WORK

Finding most of the gentry unwilling to support the repeal of the penal laws and Test Acts, some agents resorted to threats and intimidation.

About the end of April following [1688] an old acquaintance came to me to speak with me about the business of repealing the penal laws and test. ... He said that people were generally misinformed and therefore prepossessed with His Majesty's bigotry, that he was no such manner [of man] ... that neutrality was suspected both at court and in the country, that I was looked upon as one very stiff in the negative by the king, that I was represented as one particularly obstinate in this point; and that the king's eye was upon me as one likely to influence the country, &c. ... I told him that I had given him an answer the night before, which was that I gave my lord Tenham [the lord lieutenant], and desired him to insist no more on it: he was very warm and urgent with me in this business, saying that I was morose and obstinate ... not having sufficiently considered the consequence of things ...

P. C. Vellacott, 'The Diary of a Country Gentleman in 1688', *Cambridge Historical Journal*, vol. II, 1926, pp. 52–3.

DOCUMENT 10   PROPAGANDA AIMED AT THE DISSENTERS

Of all the pamphlets which aimed to exploit and increase the Dissenters' unease at being asked to support the repeal of the Test Acts in return for toleration, Halifax's Letter to a Dissenter *was perhaps the most effective.*

Consider that notwithstanding the smooth language which is now put on to engage you, these new friends [the Catholics] did not make you their choice but their refuge. They have ever made their first courtships to the Church of England, and when they were rejected there they made their application to you in the second place. ... This alliance between liberty and infallibility is bringing together the two most contrary things that are in the world. The Church of Rome doth not only dislike the allowing liberty, but by its principles it cannot do it. ... You are therefore to be hugged now, only that you may be the better squeezed at another time ...

Besides all this, you act very unskilfully against your visible interest if you throw away the advantages of which you can hardly fail in the next probable revolution [James's death and Mary's accession] ...

Halifax, [8], pp. 106, 116.

DOCUMENT 11 WILLIAM'S ATTITUDE TO REPEAL

In his efforts to win support for the repeal of the Test Acts, especially from the Dissenters, James was eager to persuade William and Mary to come out publicly in favour of repeal. When approached by Albeville, James's ambassador at the Hague, William made it clear that he supported repeal of the penal laws, but not of the Test Acts. Albeville wrote:

He told me that he had never heard or read in any history of two dominant religions at the same time in one kingdom or state; so that the Roman religion could not become dominant without the king's breaking the laws and his own promises and without (he feared) one day causing disorders which would imperil the monarchy; as for himself, he could not consent to, or approve, these proceedings of the king's and that I would find the Princess of Orange in the same sentiments and as firmly resolved as himself; that it would be better to assure the Catholics of a reasonable liberty for the present and the future than to expose them to persecution and perhaps to extirpation; for himself, he had never approved and would never approve of persecution for religion or of forcing consciences; that he would maintain the Catholics in an honest liberty, as they have in this country, but he could never agree or consent to allow them to become dominant ...

Albeville to d'Avaux, c. 17 May 1687, Public Record Office, FO 95/573.

DOCUMENT 12 BURNET'S THOUGHTS AT THE END OF 1687

Between 1686 and 1688 the historian Gilbert Burnet was in exile in Holland. His perception of events in England, largely shared by William, was heavily influenced by James's opponents.

The extremity to which the king has driven matters will throw the nation into great confusions which it will be very hard to manage. For either the nation will lose heart and then a multitude will become the feeblest thing in the world; or, if the vigour of the subjects is still kept up, it will be hard to govern this and keep it from breaking out upon great provocations, chiefly if a force is put upon the elections of Parliament men, which strikes at all.

... If the king's ill conduct throws the nation into such a violent fermentation, then a rebellion that prospers will turn to a commonwealth, and if it is subdued it will put all things in the king's hands. ... A war at home of any continuance will naturally bring over a French army, in whose hands the king will put such places as are in his power ...

Burnet, [4], pp. 261-2.

DOCUMENT 13 · WILLIAM'S DECLARATION

Designed to appeal to Tories as well as Whigs, this catalogued James's misdeeds (blamed on evil advisers, not the king himself) and proposed the one remedy on which all could agree – a free Parliament.

We cannot any longer forbear to declare that, to our great regret, we see that those counsellors who have now the chief credit with the king have overturned the religion, laws and liberties of those realms and subjected them, in all things relating to their consciences, liberties and properties, to arbitrary government. ...

But to crown all, there are great and violent presumptions inducing us to believe that those evil counsellors, in order to ... the gaining to themselves the more time ... have published that the queen hath brought forth a son; though there hath appeared, both during the queen's pretended bigness, and in the manner in which the birth was managed, so many just and visible grounds of suspicion, that not only we ourselves but all the good subjects of those kingdoms do vehemently suspect that the pretended Prince of Wales was not born by the queen. ...

We cannot excuse ourselves from espousing their [the kingdoms'] interests in a matter of such high consequence; and from contributing all that lies in us for the maintaining, both of the Protestant religion and of the laws and liberties of those kingdoms ... to the doing of which we are most earnestly solicited by a great many lords, both spiritual and temporal, and by many gentlemen and other subjects of all ranks. Therefore it is, that we have thought fit to go over to England and to carry over with us a force sufficient, by the blessing of God, to defend us from the violence of those evil counsellors ... we now think fit to declare, that this our expedition is intended for no other design but to have a free and lawful Parliament assembled as soon as is possible ...

Williams, [20], pp. 10-11, 15.

DOCUMENT 14 WILLIAM'S DEMANDS, 9 DECEMBER 1688

These make it clear that William was prepared to agree to a settlement whereby James remained king.

1. That all Papists and such persons as are not qualified by law be disarmed, disbanded and removed from all employments civil and military.

2. That all proclamations which reflect on us or [any that] have come to us, or declared for us, be recalled and that if any persons for having so assisted us have been committed, that they be forthwith set at liberty.

3. That for the security and safety of the City of London, the custody and government of the Tower be immediately put into the hands of the said City.

4. That if His Majesty should think fit to be in London during the sitting of the Parliament, that we may be there also with an equal number of guards, or if His Majesty shall be pleased to be in any place from London, at whatever distance he thinks fit, that we may be at a place of the same distance. And that the respective armies do remove from London forty miles. And that no further forces be brought into the kingdom.

5. That for the security of the City of London, and their trade, Tilbury Fort be put into the hands of the said City.

6. That to prevent the landing of French or other foreign troops, Portsmouth may be put into such hands as by Your Majesty and us shall be agreed on.

7. That some sufficient part of the public revenue be assigned us for the support and maintenance of our forces, till the meeting of a free Parliament.

Halifax, [9], vol. II, pp. 29–30.

DOCUMENT 15   **WILLIAM INSISTS ON BEING MADE KING**

Burnet tells how William broke the deadlock between the two Houses about offering the Crown to William as well as Mary.

After a reservedness that had continued so close for several weeks that nobody could certainly tell what he desired, he called for the Marquis of Halifax, the Earls of Shrewsbury and Danby and some others to explain himself more distinctly to them. ... He said no man could esteem a woman more than he did the Princess; but he was so made that he could not think of holding anything by apron strings; nor did he think it reasonable to have any share in the government unless it was put in his person and that for term of life; if they did think to settle it otherwise ... he would go back to Holland and meddle no more in their affairs. ... He could not resolve to accept of a dignity, so as to hold it only for the life of another: yet he thought that the issue of Princess Anne should be preferred in the succession to any issue that he might have by any other wife than the Princess.

Burnet, [3], vol. III, pp. 395–6.

DOCUMENT 16   BURNET'S ASSESSMENT OF WILLIAM

Burnet tries to explain why William was neither appreciated nor liked by the English.

His strength lay rather in a true discerning and a sound judgment than in imagination or invention: his designs were always great and good: but it was thought he trusted too much to that and that he did not descend enough to the humours of his people, to make himself and his notions more acceptable to them. This, in a government that has so much of freedom in it as ours, was more necessary than he was inclined to believe: his reservedness grew on him, so that it disgusted most of those who served him: but he had observed the errors of too much talking more than those of too cold a silence. He did not like contradiction nor to have his actions censured ... yet he did not love flatterers.

He knew all foreign affairs well, and understood the state of every court in Europe very particularly: he instructed his own ministers himself; but did not apply enough to affairs at home. ...

His indifference as to the forms of church-government and his being zealous for toleration, together with his cold behaviour towards the clergy, gave them generally very ill impressions of him ... He loved the Dutch, and was much beloved among them: but the ill returns he met from the English nation, their jealousies of him and their perverseness towards him, had too much soured his mind, and had in a great measure alienated him from them, which he did not take care enough to conceal, though he saw the ill effects this had upon his business. ...

I considered him as a person raised up by God to resist the power of France and the progress of tyranny and persecution. ... After all the abatements that may be allowed for his errors and faults, he ought still to be reckoned among the greatest princes that our history, or indeed that any other, can afford.

Burnet, [3], vol. IV, pp. 562–7.

DOCUMENT 17   LOCKE'S POLITICAL THEORY

Locke's Two Treatises of Government *were published, anonymously, early in 1690. Their purpose was 'to establish the throne of King William' and 'to justify to the world the people of England'. These extracts illustrate some major points in the argument.*

(a) The Original Compact

Men being ... by nature all free, equal and independent, no one can be put out of his estate and subjected to the political power of another without his own consent. The only way whereby any one divests himself of his natural liberty and puts on the bonds of civil society is by agreeing with other men to join and unite into a community, for their comfortable, safe and peaceable living one amongst another, in a secure enjoyment of their properties and a great security against any that are not of it. ... When any number of men have so consented to make one community or government, they are thereby presently incorporated and make one body politic, wherein the majority have a right to act and conclude the rest.

Locke, [14], pp. 374–5.

(b) Political power as a trust

The legislative being only a fiduciary power to act for certain ends, there remains still in the people a supreme power to remove or alter the legislative when they find the legislative act contrary to the trust reposed in them. For all power given with trust, for the attaining an end, being limited by that end, whenever that end is manifestly neglected, or opposed, the trust must necessarily be forfeited, and the power devolve into the hands of those that gave it, who may place it anew where they shall think best for their safety and security.

ibid, p. 413.

(c) The dissolution of government

Besides this overturning from without [by conquest], governments are dissolved from within. First, when the legislative is altered ... When any one, or more, shall take upon them to make laws, whom the people have not appointed so to do, they make laws without authority, which the people are not therefore bound to obey ... being in full liberty to resist the force of those who, without authority, would impose anything upon them.

When such a single person or prince sets up his own arbitrary will in place of the laws which are the will of the society, declared by the legislative, then the legislative is changed ...

ibid, pp. 455–6.

In these and the like cases when the government is dissolved, the people are at liberty to provide for themselves by erecting a new legislative, differing from the other by the change of persons, or form, or both, as they shall find it most for their safety and good ...

ibid, p. 459.

Here 'tis like, the common question will be made, who shall be judge whether the prince or legislative act contrary to their trust? ... To this I reply, the people shall be judge; for who shall be judge whether his trustee or deputy acts well and according to the trust reposed in him but he who deputes him and must, by having deputed him, have still a power to discard him when he fails in his trust? ...

ibid., p. 476.

The end of government is the good of mankind, and which is best for mankind, that the people should be always exposed to the boundless will of tyranny or that rulers should be sometimes liable to be opposed, when they grow exorbitant in the use of their power and employ it for the destruction and not the preservation of the properties of their people? ...

ibid., p. 466.

DOCUMENT 18 THE TORIES AND THE CROWN, 1689

This argument, drawn up by the Lords for use in the conference with the Commons on 6 February, shows the Tory majority's concern to maintain the hereditary principle and, less explicitly, to avoid making William king.

Although the Lords have declared that the king has deserted the government, and thereupon they have made application to the Prince of Orange to take upon him the administration of the government and thereby to provide for the peace and safety of the kingdom; yet there can be no other inference drawn from thence, but only that the exercise of the government by King James II was ceased; so as that the Lords were and are willing to secure the nation against the return of the said king into this kingdom; but not that there was either such an abdication by him or such a vacancy in the throne, as that the crown was thereby become elective. ... No act of the king alone can bar or destroy the right of his heirs to the crown; and therefore ... if the throne be vacant of King James II, allegiance is due to such person as the right of succession does belong to.

Lords Journals, vol. XIV, p. 117

DOCUMENT 19 WHIG PRAGMATISM, 1689

In these speeches from the conference on 6 February, the Whig spokesmen for the Commons based their case not on constitutional principle but on the argument that a vacuum existed at the head of the government and that it was up to the Convention to fill it.

Sir John Maynard: I am sure, if we be left without a government, as we find we are (why else have we desired the Prince to take upon him the administration?) sure we must not be perpetually under anarchy. ... All they [the Commons] mean by this matter is to provide a supply for this defect in the government brought upon it by the late king's maladministration. And I do say again, this provision must be made: and if it be, that would not make the kingdom perpetually elective ...

Sir Thomas Lee: I would ask this question, whether upon the original contract there were not a power preserved in the nation to provide for itself in such exigencies? That contract was to settle the constitution as to the legislature ... so we take it to be; and it is true that it is a part of the contract, the making of laws and that those laws should oblige all sides when made; but yet so as not to exclude this original constitution in all governments that commence by compact, that there should be a power in the states to make provision in all times and upon all occasions for extraordinary cases and necessities, such as ours now is ...

Maynard: If we look but into the law of nature (that is above all human laws) we have enough to justify us in what we are now a-doing, to provide for ourselves and the public weal in such an exigency as this ...

Parliamentary History, [16], vol. V, pp. 89, 100, 103.

DOCUMENT 20 **THE POST-REVOLUTION CONSTITUTION: CONTRACT THEORY**

The Revolution Vindicated (1689) *justifies the Revolution in terms of the 'original contract', which is seen as implicit in the ancient constitution.*

By the Original Contract was meant the agreement that had always been between the kings and people of England, that the government should be a legal government. When this agreement was first made, and the particular form and nature of it in its infancy, are things as obscure as the beginning of governments; but vestiges of it are to be found as far back as we can go, and it may be traced down through the whole history of England, and of the many wars and revolutions that have happened, to make it good, and in which kings have suffered expressly for breaking it. Besides, the thing is obvious everywhere in the frame of the government, for how came it to be a bounded limited monarchy, but that bounds and limits were agreed on? And whensoever this was first done, the Original Contract had then its rise and birth.

Kenyon, [85], p. 43.

DOCUMENT 21 **A MIXED AND BALANCED CONSTITUTION**

This extract from a Whig pamphlet from 1697 offers a traditional view of

the constitution, similar to that in Charles I's answer to the Nineteen
Propositions (Kenyon, [13], pp. 18–20).

Our constitution is a limited mixed monarchy, where the king enjoys all the
prerogatives necessary to the support of his dignity and the protection of his
people and is only abridged from the power of injuring his own subjects. ...
Lest the extraordinary power intrusted in the crown should lean towards
arbitrary government, or the tumultuary licentiousness of the people should
incline towards a democracy, the wisdom of our ancestors hath instituted a
middle state, viz. of nobility, whose interest it is to trim this boat of our
commonwealth, and to screen the people against the insults of the prince
and the prince against the popularity of the Commons ... The excellence of
this government consists in the due balance of the several constituent parts
of it ...

J. Trenchard and W. Moyle, *An Argument Showing that a Standing Army is
Inconsistent with a Free Government*, 1697, reprinted by The Rota, Exeter,
1971, pp. 2–3.

DOCUMENT 22   **HEADS OF GRIEVANCES, 7 FEBRUARY 1689**

*The first list of grievances, drawn up on 2 February, made no distinction
between heads confirming old laws and those which required fresh
legislation: see Schwoerer, [110], pp. 299–300. The first part of this
document, slightly modified, became part of the Declaration of Rights and,
after further amendments, the Bill of Rights: see Williams, [20], pp. 26–33.
The second part was dropped.*

The said Commons so elected, being now assembled in a full and free
representative of this nation, taking into their most serious consideration the
best means for attaining the ends aforesaid, do in the first place (as their
ancestors in like case have usually done) for the vindicating and asserting
their ancient rights and liberties, unanimously declare

That the pretended power of dispensing or suspending of laws, or the
execution of laws, by regal authority, without consent of Parliament, is
illegal.

That the commission for erecting the late court of commissioners for
ecclesiastical causes and all other commissions and courts of like nature are
illegal and pernicious.

That levying of money for or to the use of the crown, by pretence of
prerogative, without grant of Parliament, for longer time, or in other
manner, than the same is or shall be granted is illegal.

That it is the right of the subjects to petition the king and all
commitments and prosecutions for such petitioning are illegal.

That the raising or keeping of a standing army within the kingdom in time of peace, unless it be with consent of Parliament, is against law.

That the subjects which are Protestants may provide and keep arms for their common defence.

That election of Members of Parliament ought to be free.

That the freedom of speech and debates or proceedings in Parliament ought not to be impeached or questioned in any court or place out of Parliament.

That excessive bail ought not to be required; nor excessive fines imposed; nor cruel and unusual punishments inflicted.

That jurors ought to be duly impanelled and returned; and jurors which pass upon men in trials for high treason ought to be freeholders.

That all grants and promises of fines and forfeitures of particular persons before conviction are illegal and void.

And that for the redress of all grievances and for the amending, strengthening and preserving of the laws, Parliaments ought to be held frequently and suffered to sit ...

And towards the making a more firm and perfect settlement of the said religion, laws and liberties, it is proposed and advised ... that there be provision by new laws ... to the purposes following, viz.

For repealing the Acts concerning the militia and settling it anew;

For securing the right and freedom of electing members of the House of Commons, and the rights and privileges of Parliaments, and members thereof; as well in the intervals of Parliament as during their sitting;

For securing the frequent sitting of Parliaments;

For preventing the too long continuance of the same Parliament;

For securing universities, cities and towns corporate and boroughs and plantations against *Quo Warrantos* and surrenders and mandates and restoring them to their ancient rights;

None of the royal family to marry a Papist;

Every King and Queen of this realm at the time of their entering into the exercise of their regal authority, to take an oath for the maintaining the Protestant religion and the laws and liberties of this nation; and the coronation oath to be altered;

For the liberty of Protestants in the exercise of their religion; and for uniting all Protestants in the matter of public worship, as far as may be;

For regulating constructions upon the statutes of treasons, and trials and proceedings and writs of error in cases of treason;

For making judges' commissions *quamdiu se bene gesserint*; and ascertaining and establishing their salaries, to be paid out of the public revenue only; and for preventing their being removed and suspended from the execution of their offices, unless by due course of law;

For better securing the subjects against excessive bail in criminal cases and excessive fines and cruel and unusual punishments;

For reforming abuses in the appointing of sheriffs and in the execution of their office;

For securing the due impanelling and returning of jurors and preventing corrupt and false verdicts;

For taking away informations in the Court of King's Bench;

For regulating the Chancery and other courts of justice, and the fees of officers;

For preventing the buying and selling of offices;

For giving liberty to the subjects to traverse returns upon *habeas corpuses* and *mandamuses*;

For preventing the grants and promises of fines and forfeitures before conviction;

For redressing the abuses and oppressions in levying the hearth money;

And for redressing the abuses and oppressions in levying and collecting the excise.

Commons Journals, vol. X, pp. 21–2.

DOCUMENT 23   DEBATE ON THE KING'S REVENUES, 27 FEBRUARY 1689

Clarges and Seymour were both Tories; their speeches reflect Tory disenchantment with William, but also a concern (shared by many Whigs) to avoid the mistakes of 1660 and 1685.

Sir Thomas Clarges: I would have the monarch and the people in mutual confidence or else there is no safety to either. I think we ought to be cautious of the revenue, which is the life of the government, and consider the two last reigns. It seems, by the king's declaration, we are out of danger of falling into the misfortunes of the two last governments. If you give this revenue for three years, you will be secure of a Parliament. I doubt not the people of England, when they meet here and have good execution of their laws and are in security and safety; 'tis an unreasonable supposition that the people will not aid him according to his occasions. And I move, that the revenue may be settled for three years.

Sir Edward Seymour: What you settle on the crown I would have so well done as to support the crown and not carry it to excess. We may date our misery from our bounty here. If King Charles II had not had that bounty from you, he had never attempted what he had done.

Grey, [7], vol. IX, pp. 123, 125.

DOCUMENT 24   BURNET ON THE KING'S REVENUES

Like the Commons, William knew that the revenue was the key to the constitutional settlement.

He expressed an earnest desire to have the revenue of the crown settled on him for life: he said he was not a king till that was done: without that, the title of a king was only a pageant. And he spoke of this with more than ordinary vehemence: so that sometimes he said, he would not stay and hold an empty name, unless that was done ... he was sure that the worst of all governments was a king without treasure and without power. But a jealousy was now infused into many, that he would grow arbitrary in his government, if he once had the revenue; and would strain for a high stretch of prerogative as soon as he was out of difficulties and necessities.

Burnet, [3], vol. IV, pp. 60–1.

DOCUMENT 25 HIGH CHURCH RETREAT ON COMPREHENSION

In 1688, the Seven Bishops' petition declared a willingness 'to come to such a temper [with the Dissenters] as shall he thought fit when that matter shall be considered and settled in Parliament and Convocation'; this was followed by talks between Churchmen and Presbyterians. By January 1689, fearing that William favoured Dissent and disliked the Church, they had changed their tune, as Clarendon found when he visited Archbishop Sancroft.

He said he knew well what was in their petition, and he believed every bishop in England intended to make it good, when there was an opportunity of debating those matters in Convocation; but till then, or without a commission from the king, it was highly penal to enter upon church matters; but however he would have it in his mind and would be willing to discourse any of the bishops or other clergy thereupon, if they came to him; though he believed the Dissenters would never agree among themselves with what concessions they would be satisfied. To which Dr Tenison replied, he believed so too, that he had not discoursed with any of them upon this subject; and the way to do good was not to discourse with them, but for the bishops to endeavour to get such concessions settled in Parliament, the granting whereof (whether accepted or not by the Dissenters) should be good for the Church.

Clarendon, [5], vol. II, p. 240.

DOCUMENT 26 ARGUMENTS FOR AND AGAINST COMPREHENSION

A committee of divines was ordered to draw up a list of possible changes to the Prayer Book, to be laid before Convocation.

... the most rigid ... thought too much was already done for the Dissenters in the toleration that was granted them ... that the altering the customs and constitution of our church to gratify a peevish and obstinate party was like to have no other effect on them, but to make them more insolent; as if the Church, by offering these alterations, seemed to confess that she had been hitherto in the wrong ... in answer to all this it was said that if by a few corrections or explanations we offered all just satisfaction to the chief objections of the Dissenters, we had reason to hope that this would bring over many of them ... The toleration now granted seemed to render it more necessary than formerly to make the terms of communion with the Church as large as might be; that so we might draw over to us the greater number from those who might now leave us more safely ...

Burnet, [3], vol. IV, pp. 55–7.

DOCUMENT 27 THE RISE OF THE MONIED INTEREST: BOLINGBROKE IN 1709

This letter, to Lord Orrery, sets out the Tory claim that the wars had destroyed the old pre-eminence of land and created a new form of wealth, morally inferior and politically subversive.

We have been twenty years engaged in the two most expensive wars that Europe ever saw. The whole burden of this charge has lain upon the landed interest during the whole time. The men of estates have, generally speaking, neither served in the fleets nor armies, nor meddled in the public funds and management of the treasure.

A new interest has been created out of their fortunes, and a new sort of property which was not known twenty years ago is now increased to be almost equal to the terra firma of our island. The consequence of all is, that the landed men are become poor and dispirited. They either abandon all thoughts of the public, turn arrant farmers and improve the estates they have left; or else they seek to repair their shattered fortunes by listing at court, or under the heads of parties. In the mean while those men are become their masters, who formerly would with joy have been their servants. To judge therefore rightly of what turn our domestic affairs are in any respect likely to take, we must for the future only consider what the temper of the Court and of the Bank is.

Holmes and Speck, [11], pp. 135–6.

DOCUMENT 28   A LOW CHURCHMAN'S CREED: THOMAS PAPILLON

Of Huguenot descent, Papillon adhered to the Puritan tradition. Writing (probably) in the 1680s, he used 'Tory' and 'Whig' where twenty years later he would have referred to 'High' and 'Low' Church – but by then the Low Church had become mainly Latitudinarian.

The kingdom of England is made up of Papists and Protestants. The Protestants are divided, and of late years distinguished by the names of Tories and Whigs. Under the name of Tories is comprehended all those that cry up the Church of England in opposition to the Churches of Christ in foreign parts, that press the forms and ceremonies more than the doctrines of the Church, which are sound and Scriptural; and that either in their own practice are swearers, drunkards or loose in their conversation, or do allow of and are unwilling such should be punished, but give them all countenance provided they stickle for forms and ceremonies and rail against and endeavour to discountenance all those that are otherwise minded.

Under the name of Whigs is comprehended most of the sober and religious persons of the Church of England that sincerely embrace the doctrines of the Church, and put no such stress on the forms and ceremonies, but look on them as human institutions, and not as the essentials of religion, and are willing that there might be a reformation to take away offence, and that desire that all swearing, drunkenness and ungodliness should be discountenanced and punished, and do own the foreign Protestant Churches as Churches of Christ, and hold communion with them. As also all dissenters of the several persuasions are included under this title ...

A.F.W. Papillon, *Memoirs of Thomas Papillon of London, Merchant*, Reading, 1887, pp. 374–6.

DOCUMENT 29   THE DEMAND FOR THE RECALL OF CONVOCATION, 1697

Francis Atterbury's Letter to a Convocation Man *sets out the view that the Church was in danger.*

If ever there was need of a Convocation, since Christianity was established in this kingdom, there is need of one now: when such an open looseness in men's principles and practices and such a settled contempt of religion and the priesthood have prevailed everywhere; when heresies of all kinds, when scepticism, deism and atheism itself overrun us like a deluge; when the Mosaic history has by men of our own order been cunningly undermined and exposed, under pretence of explaining it; when the Trinity has been as openly denied by some as the Unity of the Godhead sophistically opposed by others; when all mysteries in religion have been decried as impositions on men's understandings, and nothing is admitted as an article of faith but what we can fully and perfectly comprehend; nay, when the power of the Magistrate and of the Church is struck at, and the indifference of all religions is endeavoured to be established by pleas for the justice and necessity of an universal toleration, even against the sense of the whole legislature. At such a time and in such an age, you and I, Sir, and all men that wish well to the interests of religion and the state cannot but think that there is great need of a Convocation.

Holmes and Speck, [11], p. 116.

DOCUMENT 30   THE LATITUDINARIAN OUTLOOK: JOHN TILLOTSON

This sermon argues that God is not severe and wrathful, but kind and undemanding.

One of the great prejudices which men have entertained against the Christian religion is this, that it lays upon men heavy burdens and grievous to be borne, that the laws of it are very strict and severe, difficult to be kept and yet dangerous to be broken. ... For the removal of this prejudice I have chosen these words of the apostle, which expressly tell us the contrary, that the commandments of God are not grievous. ... Upon this account it will be requisite to take some pains to satisfy the reason of men concerning this truth, and if possible make it so evident that those who are unwilling to own it may yet be ashamed to deny it. And methinks I have this peculiar advantage of the argument that I have now undertaken, that every reasonable man cannot but choose to wish me success in this attempt, because I undertake the proof of that which it is every man's interest that it should be true ...

N. Sykes, *From Sheldon to Secker*, Cambridge University Press, 1959, p. 151.

DOCUMENT 31   STATUTORY LIMITATIONS ON THE CROWN: THE ACT OF SETTLEMENT, 1701

Although the immediate purpose of this Act was to ensure that Anne would be succeeded by the House of Hanover, its full title was 'An Act for the further limitation of the crown and better securing the rights and liberties of the subject'. It reflected the widespread belief that William had sacrificed English to foreign interests and the fear that a future German king might do the same.

And whereas it is requisite and necessary that some further provision be made for securing our religion, laws and liberties, from and after the death of his Majesty and the princess Anne of Denmark ... be it enacted ...

That whosoever shall hereafter come to the possession of this crown, shall join in communion with the Church of England, as by law established.

That in case the crown and imperial dignity of this realm shall hereafter come to any person, not being a native of this kingdom of England, this nation be not obliged to engage in any war for the defence of any dominions or territories which do not belong to the crown of England, without the consent of Parliament.

That no person who shall hereafter come to the possession of this crown, shall go out of the dominions of England, Scotland or Ireland, without consent of Parliament.

That from and after the time that the further limitation by this act shall take effect, all matters and things relating to the well governing of this kingdom, which are properly cognizable in the privy council by the laws and customs of this realm, shall be transacted there, and all resolutions taken thereupon shall be signed by such of the privy council as shall advise and consent to the same.

That after the said limitation shall take effect as aforesaid, no person born out of the kingdoms of England, Scotland or Ireland, or the dominions thereunto belonging (although he be naturalized or made a denizen, except such as are born of English parents) shall be capable to be of the privy council, or a member of either house of parliament, or to enjoy any office or place of trust, either civil or military, or to have any grant of lands, tenements or hereditaments from the crown, to himself or to any other or others in trust for him.

That no person who has an office or place of profit under the King, or receives a pension from the crown, shall be capable of serving as a member of the House of Commons.

That after the said limitation shall take effect as aforesaid, judges' commissions be made *quamdiu se bene gesserint*, and their salaries ascertained and established; but upon the address of both houses of parliament it may be lawful to remove them.

That no pardon under the great seal of England be pleadable to an impeachment by the Commons in Parliament.

Williams, [20], pp. 58–9.

DOCUMENT 32   QUEEN ANNE ON THE THREAT OF PARTY
RULE

*This letter was written to Godolphin in August 1706, as the Whig leaders
used their majority in the Commons to put pressure on the queen to admit
them to office.*

All I desire is my liberty in encouraging and employing all those that concur
faithfully in my service, whether they are called Whigs or Tories, not to be
tied to one, or to the other, for if I should be so unfortunate as to fall into
the hands of either, I shall look upon myself, though I have the name of
Queen, to be in reality but their slave, which as it will be my personal ruin,
so it will be the destroying of all government, for instead of putting an end
to faction, it will lay a lasting foundation for it ...

Why for God's sake must I who have no interest, no end, no thought but
for the good of my country, be made so miserable as to be brought into the
power of one set of men, and why may I not be trusted, since I mean
nothing but what is equally for the good of all my subjects?

Gregg, [61], p. 223.

DOCUMENT 33   PRESSURE ON QUEEN ANNE TO DISMISS
HARLEY

*By 1708 the Whig leaders had forced their way into office. Now they put
pressure on the Queen, through Godolphin and the Duke and Duchess of
Marlborough (the Duchess being a rabid Whig), to dismiss her Tory
Secretary of State, Robert Harley.*

Lord Treasurer [Godolphin] told the Queen he came to resign the staff, that
serving her longer with one so perfidious as Mr Harley was impossible; she
replied in respect of his long service, she would give him till tomorrow to
consider, when he should do as he pleased withal [;] she could find enough
glad of that staff

Then came Lady Duchess with great duty and submission, that she had
served her ever with affection and tenderness, &c, her utmost had been her
duty and she had been faithful in it. The reply is said to be, 'You shall
consider of this till tomorrow, then if you desire it, you shall have leave to
retire as you desire ... '

Then entered the Duke, prepared with his utmost address. He told her he
had ever served her with obedience and fidelity ... that he must lament he
came in competition with so vile a creature as Harley; that his fidelity and
duty should continue as long as his breath. That it was his duty to be
speedy in resigning his commands, that she might put the sword into some

other hand immediately, and it was also his duty to tell her he feared the Dutch would immediately on the news make a peace very injurious for England.

'And then, my lord,' says she, 'will you resign me your sword [?]' 'Let me tell you,' says he. 'Your service I have regarded to the utmost of my power.' 'And if you do, my lord, resign your sword, let me tell you, you will run it through my head.'

She went to Council, begging him to follow, he refusing ...

Gregg, [61], pp. 258–9.

DOCUMENT 34   MINISTERIAL PRESSURE ON GEORGE II, 1744

This discussion between George II and Lord Chancellor Hardwicke shows how ministers sought to persuade the king to endorse their policies by arguing that these were in his own best interests.

King: I have done all you asked of me. I have put all power into your hands and I suppose you will make the most of it.

Chancellor: The disposition of places is not enough if your Majesty takes pains to show the world that you disapprove of your own work.

King: My work! I was forced: I was threatened.

Chancellor: I am sorry to hear your Majesty use those expressions. I know of no force: I know of no threats. No means were used but what has been used in all times, the humble advice of your servants, supported by such reasons as convinced them that the measure was necessary for your service.

King: Yes, I was told I should be opposed.

Chancellor: Never by me, Sir, nor by any of my friends. How others might misrepresent us, I don't pretend to know; but whatever had been our fate, and though Your Majesty had decided on the contrary side to what you did, we would never have gone into an opposition against the necessary measures for carrying on the war and for the support of your government and family. ... Taking your money only is not serving you, and nothing can enable one to do that but being put into a possibility and capacity of doing so by your gracious countenance and support. ... Your ministers, Sir, are only your instruments of government.

King (smiles): Ministers are the kings in this country.

Costin and Watson, [6], vol. I, pp. 375–6.

DOCUMENT 35   WALPOLE'S ADVICE ON MANAGING
GEORGE II, 1743

Having lost office, Walpole told Henry Pelham of the methods he had used to persuade the king.

This leads me to the most tender and delicate part of the whole; I mean, your behaviour and your manner of treating this subject with him. It is a great misfortune that you have not time; for time and address have often carried things that met, at first onset, with great reluctance; and you must expect to meet the king instructed and greatly prepared in favour of the points which Carteret has in view to drive. Address and management are the weapons you must fight and defend with: plain truths will not be relished at first, in opposition to prejudices conceived and infused in favour of his own partialities; and you must dress up all you offer with the appearance of no other view or tendency but to promote his service in his own way to the utmost of your power. And the more you can make anything appear to be his own, and agreeable to his declarations and orders, given to you before he went, the better you will be heard ...

Williams, [20], pp. 80–1.

DOCUMENT 36   THE PELHAMS' CONDITIONS FOR
RETURNING TO OFFICE, 1746

Frustrated that George II paid more heed to Lords Bath and Granville than to them, his ministers (led by Henry Pelham and his brother, the Duke of Newcastle) resigned. When Bath and Granville failed to establish a majority in the Commons, George had to take the Pelhams back. They made the following stipulations before resuming office.

That out of duty to the king and regard to the public, it is apprehended that His Majesty's late servants cannot return into his service without being honoured with that degree of authority, confidence and credit from His Majesty, which the ministers of the crown have usually enjoyed in this country and which is absolutely necessary for carrying on his service. That His Majesty will be pleased entirely to withdraw his confidence and countenance from those persons who of late have, behind the curtain, suggested private counsels, with the view of creating difficulties to his servants, who are responsible for everything, whilst those persons are responsible for nothing.

That His Majesty will be pleased to demonstrate his conviction of mind that those persons have deceived or misled him, by representing that they had sufficient credit and interest in the nation to support and carry on the public affairs, and that he finds they are not able to do it.

That in order to those ends His Majesty will be pleased to remove [certain named persons].

That he will be graciously pleased to perfect the scheme lately humbly proposed to him for bringing Mr Pitt into some honourable employment, and also the other persons formerly named with him.

That His Majesty will be pleased to dispose of the vacant Garters in such manner as to strengthen, and give a public mark of his satisfaction in, his administration.

That, as to foreign affairs, His Majesty will be pleased not to require more from his servants than to support and perfect the plan which he has already approved.

Owen, [102], pp. 298–9.

DOCUMENT 37   'COUNTRY' SUSPICIONS OF WASTE AND
MISMANAGEMENT, 1689

In this debate Tories (Clarges) and Whigs (Garroway) showed their distrust of official spokesmen and the military and a fondness for unsubstantiated allegations.

Sir Thomas Clarges: I think forty thousand men may be taken out of this establishment; I am sure a less number conquered Ireland in 1650. I profess I am much in the dark till I hear some proposition of the king of the state of the war for the next year and till we know the obligation of alliances. The Dutch forces are given in fourteen thousand. They are not all in Ireland, some are in Scotland. They are upon parole to keep up 70 in a company &c and perhaps they are but 32 in a company ...

[The Earl of Ranelagh, Paymaster of the Army, gave an account of the establishment, correcting Clarges' errors.]

William Garroway: I see no certainty of the number of men in England, Scotland and Ireland. I think the account that has been transferred to you comes from the muster-master and the king is abused. I would go on regularly to the state of the war, what the king thinks fitting and they to bring in where the men are; without the certain number of men, you know not how to provide. I think it fitter to apply to the fleet and retrench the land men. England knows no need of them. I believe the money is not all spent. I think it may be embezzled. I never saw a worse account. ... I would have accounts brought here by somebody that will allow them, but I desire not to go blindfold. Let the money be rightly applied and I will go with the highest and I desire the king to give us the state of the war.

Grey, [7], vol. IX, pp. 389–90.

DOCUMENT 38 'COUNTRY' SUSPICION OF PLACEMEN, 1691

Thompson was at this time one of the most forthright 'Country' speakers among the Whigs. Although he held office for a while under William, his 'Country' principles led him to become a somewhat idiosyncratic Tory under Anne.

Sir John Thompson: I could wish we had a self-denying ordinance 'that no persons should sit here that have places or offices of profit'. I am justified by good authority; for before Henry VIII's time, no person that belonged to the court was permitted to sit within these walls. 'Tis wonderful to consider that, when the Commons were poorer than now, they should remove great men and favourites from the crown. The reason then was, there was no dependency upon the court; they brought more of the country and less of the court with them [than] in after times. I speak my mind truly and have no reserves, but I believe we shall not carry this, because there were never more dependencies on the court than now.

Grey, [7], vol. X, p. 215.

DOCUMENT 39 'COUNTRY' HOSTILITY TO STANDING ARMIES, 1697

After the Peace of Ryswick, William wished to keep up the forces raised for the war, because he believed that war would soon break out over the Spanish succession. 'Country' MPs, both Whig and Tory, claimed that he wished to use the army to make himself absolute. The standing army controversy caused the most serious political crisis of the reign and provoked a flood of pamphlets, this one written by two Whigs.

Our constitution depending upon a due balance between King, Lords and Commons, and that balance depending upon the mutual occasions and necessities they have of one another, if this cement be once broke, there is an actual dissolution of the government. Now this balance can never be preserved but by an union of the natural and artificial strength of the kingdom, that is, by making the militia to consist of the same persons as have the property; or otherwise the government is violent and against nature and cannot possibly continue, but the constitution must either break the army or the army will destroy the constitution: for it is universally true that wherever the militia is, there is or will be the government in a short time ...

The detestable policies of the last reigns were with the utmost art and application to disarm the people and make the militia useless, to countenance a standing army in order to bring in Popery and slavery ...

Why may not the nobility, gentry and freeholders of England be trusted with the defence of their own lives, estates and liberties, without having guardians and keepers assigned them? And why may they not defend them with as much vigour and courage as mercenaries who have nothing to lose? ...

J. Trenchard and W. Moyle, *An Argument Showing that a Standing Army is Inconsistent with a Free Government*, 1697, reprinted by The Rota, Exeter, 1971, pp. 4, 20–1.

DOCUMENT 40   THE TORIES' MOTIVES ON COMING TO POWER IN 1710

Bolingbroke recalls how the pursuit of power and profit and the pursuit of principle reinforced one another and argues that, under Anne, the Tories were the natural majority party.

I am afraid that we came to court in the same dispositions as all parties have done; that the principal spring of our actions was to have the government of the state in our hands; that our principal views were the conservation of this power, great employments to ourselves, and great opportunities of rewarding those who had helped to raise us, and of hurting those who stood in opposition to us. It is however true, that with these considerations of private and party interest there were others intermingled, which had for their object the public good of the nation, at least what we took to be such.

We looked on the political principles which had generally prevailed in our government from the Revolution in 1688 to be destructive of our true interest, to have mingled us too much in the affairs of the continent, to tend to the impoverishing our people and to the loosening the bands of our constitution in Church and State. We supposed the Tory party to be the bulk of the landed interest, and to have no contrary influence blended into its composition. We supposed the Whigs to be the remains of a party, formed against the ill designs of the Court under King Charles II, nursed up into strength and applied to contrary uses by King William III, and yet still so weak as to lean for support on the Presbyterians and other sectaries, on the Bank and the other corporations, on the Dutch and the other allies. From hence we judged it to follow that they had been forced, and must continue so, to render the national interest subservient to the interest of those who lent them an additional strength, without which they could never be the prevalent party. The view, therefore, of those amongst us who thought in this manner, was to improve the queen's favour to break the body of the Whigs, to render their supports useless to them and to fill the employments of the kingdom, down to the meanest, with Tories.

Holmes and Speck, [11], pp. 141–2.

DOCUMENT 41   EXPLOITATION OF 'COUNTRY'
SENSIBILITIES FOR PARTY ENDS, 1692

*This debate shows how Whig politicians tried to blame naval miscarriages
on the Tory Earl of Nottingham's allegedly lukewarm commitment to
William's regime, stigmatising his administrative shortcomings as political
disloyalty and exploiting 'Country' resentment of naval failure. It also
showed that in mixed ministries 'colleagues' had few qualms about
attacking one another.*

John Smith: .. There is a coolness in people's minds to this government
which arises, I think, because they believe you have not a rightful king but
only *de facto* and that if King James comes back they may return to their
allegiance to him. Hence arises your mischief and this, I think, ought to be
your first head of advice.

Thomas Wharton, Comptroller of the Household: The gentleman that spoke
last has touched upon the true cause of your grievance; it lies deeper than
you are aware of. Your chief men that manage matters are such as submit
to this king upon wrong principles – because he has the governing power –
but will be as ready to join another if he prevails. They are such as came
not into your government till it was late, and I think it no policy to take
men into a government because they were violent against it. I would not at
present name these persons but I would address His Majesty against them in
general (for he knows them best) and that he would be pleased to receive
such men only under him who are of known integrity and will come up
both to the principles and His Majesty's right to this government ...

    A motion was made by the friends to the Lord Nottingham that all the
papers and letters relating to the descent might be laid before this House.
But it was opposed by his enemies, the Whigs; so carried in the negative.

Luttrell, [15], pp. 274, 277.

DOCUMENT 42   A TORY'S REASONS FOR SWEARING
ALLEGIANCE TO WILLIAM

*Tories like Sir John Bramston had very mixed feelings in 1689. They did
not want their rightful king (James) to return, but were reluctant to
recognise William as king de jure. Most were prepared to swear allegiance
to William as king de facto: government had to be carried on by someone.
(See Document 19.)*

I did think, as the circumstances of the government then were, by the King
James leaving the kingdom as he did without any commission or care taken
for preservation of his subjects, private men, if required upon penalties,
might safely swear to the oath of allegiance prescribed. ... By the king

absenting himself and leaving the kingdom without any governor or commissioner, it was impossible for us to pay allegiance to him according to our oath, which oath therefore is become as to us abrogated, or at least during his absence is in abeyance. ... We that are private persons cannot judge whether his absence be voluntary or forced. ... By his absence it became necessary that government should be by somebody, to avoid confusion. There can be no government without submission to it, that can, whether by one or more, have no assurance of submission but by a religious tie and obligation; the constant practice in all states is by oath to oblige obedience. When the government is fixed, obedience becomes necessary to it, and conscience obliges private persons to yield obedience, as well as prudence and safety to prevent anarchy, and the rabble from spoiling and robbing the noble and wealthy. These assertions and reasons seem to me to arise out of pure necessity.

Autobiography of Sir John Bramston, ed. Lord Braybrooke, Camden Society, 1845, p. 355.

DOCUMENT 43   MODIFICATION OF TORY VIEWS ON NON-RESISTANCE

The Tory argument that submission was due to a king de facto *implied that submission was due to any established regime, as can be seen in this extract from a sermon of 1700.*

That there is such a submission due from all subjects to the Supreme Authority of the place wherein they live, as shall tie up their hands from opposing or resisting it by force, is evident from the very nature and ends of political society. And I dare say there is not that country on earth, let the form of government be what it will (Absolute Monarchy, Legal Monarchy, Aristocracy or Commonwealth) where this is not a part of the constitution. Subjects must obey passively where they cannot obey actively, otherwise the government would be precarious, and the public peace at the mercy of every malcontent, and a door would be set open to all the insurrections, rebellions and treasons in the world.

Kenyon, [84], p. 54.

DOCUMENT 44   RIVAL VIEWS ON FOREIGN POLICY, 1692

Clarges and Wharton state the Tory and Whig positions on foreign policy.

Sir Thomas Clarges: Why we should be at a greater charge than our treaties oblige us to, I see no reason for. I know it is a received opinion with the

Dutch and the Germans that England is an inexhaustible fountain, but if you go on at the rate you have I am afraid you will quickly be drawn dry. The security of this nation, with our interest, lies in having a good fleet at sea and, if we can, to destroy that of our enemies, and not to send armies abroad, which will drain the nation both of our people and our money too ...

Goodwin Wharton: Consider with yourself; if he [Louis XIV] swallows Flanders, Holland must follow and if France be once master of Holland, pray think what will become of you. Will your fleet be able to deal with that of France and Holland too, for that will be the consequence?

Luttrell, [15], pp. 288, 291.

DOCUMENT 45   THE CLAIM OF RIGHT, 1689

Clearly based on the English Declaration of Rights, this recorded the change of ruler and denounced various actions of James VII as illegal. It went further in declaring that James had forfeited his right to the Scottish throne and in demanding a change of church government; it also went closer than the English version to making the offer of the crown explicitly conditional on the king's respecting his subjects' rights.

Whereas King James VII, being a professed Papist, did assume the regal power and acted as king without ever taking the oath required by law, whereby the king at his access to the government is obliged to swear to maintain the Protestant religion and to rule the people according to the laudable laws; and did by the advice of wicked and evil counsellors invade the fundamental constitution of this kingdom, and altered it from a legal, limited monarchy to an arbitrary and despotic power ... and hath exercised the same to the subversion of the Protestant religion and the violation of the laws and liberties of the kingdom, inverting all the ends of government, whereby he hath forfeited the right to the crown and the throne is become vacant ...

[The Estates declare] that prelacy and the superiority of any office in the Church above presbyters is and hath been a great and insupportable grievance and trouble to this nation and contrary to the inclinations of the generality of the people since the Reformation (they having reformed from popery by the presbyters) and therefore ought to be abolished ...

Having therefore an entire confidence that his said Majesty, the king of England, will perfect the deliverance so far advanced by him and will still preserve them from the violation of their rights which they have here asserted, and from all other attempts upon their religion laws and liberties, the said Estates of the kingdom of Scotland do resolve that William and Mary ... be declared king and queen of Scotland ...

Browning, [2], pp. 635–8.

BIBLIOGRAPHY

PRIMARY SOURCES

1 Beddard, R. (ed.), *A Kingdom without a King: The Journal of the Provisional Government in the Revolution of 1688*, Phaidon, 1982.

2 Browning, A. (ed.), *English Historical Documents, 1660–1714*, Eyre & Spottiswoode, 1953.

3 Burnet, G., *History of My Own Time*, 6 vols, Oxford University Press, 1833.

4 Burnet, G., *Supplement to Burnet's History of My Own Time*, ed. H.C. Foxcroft, Oxford University Press, 1902.

5 Clarendon, Earl of (H. Hyde), *Correspondence and Diaries*, ed. S.W. Singer, 2 vols, London, 1828.

6 Costin, W.C. and Watson, J.S. (eds), *The Law and Working of the Constitution*, vol. I, 1660–1783, Black, 1952.

7 Grey, A., *Debates in the House of Commons, 1667–94*, 10 vols, London, 1769.

8 Halifax, Marquis of (G. Savile), *Complete Works*, ed. J.P. Kenyon, Penguin, 1969.

9 Halifax, Marquis of (G. Savile), *Life and Letters*, ed. H.C. Foxcroft, 2 vols, Longman, 1898.

10 Hardwicke, Earl of (P. Yorke), *Miscellaneous State Papers*, 2 vols., 1778.

11 Holmes, G. and Speck, W.A. (eds), *The Divided Society: Parties and Politics in England, 1694–1716*, Arnold, 1967.

12 Jones, D.L. (ed.), *A Parliamentary History of the Glorious Revolution*, HMSO, 1988 [includes 18, 19 and material from 7].

13 Kenyon, J.P., *The Stuart Constitution*, 2nd edn, Cambridge University Press, 1986.

14 Locke, J., *Two Treatises of Government*, ed. P. Laslett, Mentor, 1965.

15 Luttrell, N., *Parliamentary Diary, 1691–3*, ed. H. Horwitz, Oxford University Press, 1972.

16 *Parliamentary History*, ed. W. Cobbett, vol. V, 1688–1702, London, 1809.

17 Reresby, Sir J., *Memoirs*, ed. A. Browning, revised by M.K. Geiter and W.A. Speck, Royal Historical Society, 1991.

18 Schwoerer, L.G., 'A Jornall of the Convention at Westminster Begun

the 22 of January, 1688/9', *Bulletin of the Institute of Historical Research*, vol. XLIX, 1976.

19 Simpson, A., 'Notes of a Noble Lord, 22 January to 12 February, 1689', *English Historical Review*, vol. LII, 1937.

20 Williams, E.N., *The Eighteenth Century Constitution*, Cambridge University Press, 1960.

SECONDARY WORKS

21 Ashcraft, R., *Revolutionary Politics and Locke's 'Two Treatises of Government'*, Princeton University Press, 1986.

22 Barnard, T.C., 'Crises of Identity among Irish Protestants, 1641–85', *Past and Present*, no. 127, 1990.

23 Baxter, S., *William III*, Longman, 1966.

24 Beattie, J.M., *Crime and the Courts, 1660–1800*, Oxford University Press, 1986.

25 Beckett, J.V., 'Land Tax or Excise: The Levying of Taxation in the Seventeenth and Eighteenth Centuries', *English Historical Review*, vol. C, 1985.

26 Beddard, R. (ed.), *The Revolutions of 1688*, Oxford University Press, 1991.

27 Bennett, G.V., 'The Seven Bishops: a Reconsideration' in D. Baker (ed.), *Religious Motivation*, Studies in Church History, vol. XV, Blackwell, 1978.

28 Bennett, G.V., *The Tory Crisis in Church and State, 1688–1730*, Oxford University Press, 1975.

29 Bolam, C.G., Goring, J.J., Short, H.L. and Thomas, R., *The English Presbyterians*, Allen & Unwin, 1968.

30 Borsay, P., *The English Urban Renaissance: Culture and Society in the English Town, 1660–1770*, Oxford University Press, 1989.

31 Braddick, M.J., *The Nerves of State: Taxation and the Financing of the British State, 1558–1714*, Manchester University Press, 1996.

32 Bradshaw, B. and Morrill, J.S. (eds), *The British Problem, c.1534–1707*, Macmillan, 1996.

33 Brewer, J., *The Sinews of Power: War, Money and the English State, 1689–1783*, Unwin Hyman, 1989.

34 Brooks, C., 'The Country Persuasion and Political Responsibility in England in the 1690s', *Parliaments, Estates and Representation*, vol. 4, 1988.

35 Brooks, C., 'Public Finance and Political Stability: The Administration of the Land Tax, 1688–1720', *Historical Journal*, vol. XVII, 1974.

36 Brown, K., *Kingdom or Province? Scotland and the Regal Union, 1603–1715*, Macmillan, 1992.

37 Cannon, J., *Aristocratic Century: The Peerage of Eighteenth-Century England*, Cambridge University Press, 1984.

38 Childs, J., *The Army, James II and the Glorious Revolution*, Manchester University Press, 1980.

39 Childs, J., '1688', *History*, vol. LXXIII, 1988.

40 Clark, J.C.D., *English Society, 1688–1832*, Cambridge University Press, 1985.

41 Clark, J.C.D., *Revolution and Rebellion: State and Society in England in the Seventeenth and Eighteenth Centuries*, Cambridge University Press, 1986.

42 Colley, L., *In Defiance of Oligarchy: The Tory Party, 1714–60*, Cambridge, 1982.

43 Connolly, S.J., *Religion, Law and Power: The Making of Protestant Ireland, 1660–1760*, Oxford University Press, 1992.

44 Corfield, P.J., 'Class by name and number in Eighteenth-century England', *History*, vol. LXXII, 1987.

45 Corfield, P.J., *The Impact of English Towns, 1700–1800*, Oxford University Press, 1982.

46 Cruickshanks, E. (ed.), *By Force or by Default? The Revolution of 1688–89*, John Donald, 1989.

47 Cruickshanks, E. and Black, J. (eds), *The Jacobite Challenge*, John Donald, 1988.

48 Curtis, T.C. and Speck, W.A., 'The Societies for the Reformation of Manners', *Literature and History*, vol. III, 1976.

49 De Krey, G.S., *A Fractured Society: The Politics of London in the First Age of Party, 1688–1715*, Oxford University Press, 1985.

50 Dickinson, H.T., *Liberty and Property: Political Ideology in Eighteenth-Century Britain*, Methuen, 1979.

51 Dickinson, H.T., *The Politics of the People in Eighteenth-Century Britain*, Macmillan, 1994.

52 Dickson, P.G.M., *The Financial Revolution in England, 1688–1756*, Macmillan, 1967.

53 Downie, J.A., 'The Commission of Public Accounts and the Formation of the Country Party', *English Historical Review*, vol. XCI, 1976.

54 Earle, P., *The Making of the English Middle Class, 1660–1730*, Methuen, 1989.

55 Feiling, K.G., *History of the Tory Party, 1640–1714*, Oxford University Press, 1924.

56 Ferguson, W., *Scotland, 1689 to the Present*, Oliver & Boyd, 1968.

57 Frankle, R.J., 'The Formulation of the Declaration of Rights', *Historical Journal*, vol. XVII, 1974.

58 Glassey, L., *Politics and the Appointment of Justices of the Peace, 1675–1720*, Oxford University Press, 1979.

59 Goldie, M., 'The Political Thought of the Anglican Revolution', in Beddard, R. (ed.), *Revolutions of 1688*, Oxford University Press, 1991.

60 Goldie, M., 'The Roots of True Whiggism, 1688–94', *History of Political Thought*, vol. I, 1980.

61 Gregg, E., *Queen Anne*, Routledge & Kegan Paul, 1980.
62 Grell, O.P., Israel, J.I. and Tyacke, N. (eds) *From Persecution to Toleration: The Glorious Revolution and Religion in England*, Oxford University Press, 1991.
63 Harris, T., *Politics under the later Stuarts*, 1660–1715, Longman, 1993.
64 Havighurst, A.F., 'James II and the Twelve Men in Scarlet', *Law Quarterly Review*, vol. LXIX, 1953.
65 Hay, D., 'Property, Authority and the Criminal Law', in D. Hay, P. Linebaugh, J.G. Rule, E.P. Thompson and C. Winslow (eds), *Albion's Fatal Tree: Crime and Society in Eighteenth-century England*, Allen Lane, 1975.
66 Hayton, D., 'The "Country" Interest and the Party System' in C. Jones (ed.), *Party and Management in Parliament, 1660–1784*, Leicester University Press, 1984.
67 Hayton, D., 'Moral Reform and Country Politics in the late Seventeenth-century House of Commons', *Past and Present*, no. 128, 1990.
68 Hoak, D. and Feingold, M. (eds.), *The World of William and Mary: Anglo-Dutch Perspectives on the Revolution of 1688*, Stanford University Press, 1996.
69 Holmes, G. (ed.), *Britain after the Glorious Revolution, 1689–1714*, Macmillan, 1969.
70 Holmes, G., *British Politics in the Age of Anne*, revised edn, Hambledon, 1987.
71 Holmes, G., *The Electorate and the National Will in the First Age of Party*, Inaugural Lecture, Lancaster, 1975.
72 Holmes, G., *The Trial of Dr Sacheverell*, Methuen, 1973.
73 Horwitz, H., 'Parliament and the Glorious Revolution', *Bulletin of the Institute of Historical Research*, vol. XLVII, 1974.
74 Horwitz, H., *Parliament, Policy and Politics in the Reign of William III*, Manchester University Press, 1977.
75 Horwitz, H., *Revolution Politicks: The Career of Daniel Finch, Second Earl of Nottingham*, Cambridge University Press, 1968.
76 Horwitz, H., '1689 (and all that)', *Parliamentary History*, vol. VI, 1987.
77 Hosford, D.H., *Nottingham, Nobles and the North: Aspects of the Revolution of 1688*, Archon, 1976.
78 Israel, J.I. (ed.), *The Anglo-Dutch Moment: Essays on the Glorious Revolution and its World Impact*, Cambridge University Press, 1991.
79 Jones, C. (ed.), *Britain in the first Age of Party, 1680–1750*, Hambledon, 1987.
80 Jones, D.W., *War and Economy in the Age of William III and Marlborough*, Blackwell, 1988.
81 Jones, J.R. (ed.), *Liberty Secured? Britain before and after 1688*, Stanford University Press, 1992.

82 Jones, J.R., *The Revolution of 1688 in England*, Weidenfeld & Nicolson, 1972.
83 Kent, J., 'The Centre and the Localities: State formation and parish government in England, c. 1640–1740', *Historical Journal*, vol. XXXVIII, 1995.
84 Kenyon, J.P., 'The Revolution of 1688: Resistance and Contract', in N. McKendrick (ed.), *Historical Perspectives: Studies in English Thought and Society in Honour of J.H. Plumb*, Europa, 1974.
85 Kenyon, J.P., *Revolution Principles: The Politics of Party, 1689–1720*, Cambridge University Press, 1977.
86 Kenyon, J.P., *Robert Spencer, Earl of Sunderland*, Longman, 1958.
87 Landau, N., *The Justices of the Peace, 1679–1760*, California University Press, 1984.
88 Langbein, J. H., 'Albion's Fatal Flaws', *Past and Present*, no. 98, 1983.
89 Langford, P., *The Excise Crisis*, Oxford, 1975.
90 Macaulay, T.B., *History of England*, ed. C.H. Firth, 6 vols, Macmillan, 1913.
91 Mathias, P. and O'Brien, P., 'Taxation in Britain and France, 1715–1810', *Journal of European Economic History*, vol. V, 1976.
92 McKendrick, N., Brewer, J. and Plumb, J.H., *The Birth of a Consumer Society*, Europa, 1982.
93 Miller, J., 'The Crown and the Borough Charters in the Reign of Charles II', *English Historical Review*, vol. C, 1985.
94 Miller, J., 'The Glorious Revolution: "Contract" and "Abdication" Reconsidered', *Historical Journal*, vol. XXV, 1982.
95 Miller, J., *James II: A Study in Kingship*, Methuen, 1989.
96 Miller, J., 'William III: The English View', in B. Whelan (ed.) *The Last of the Great Wars*, Limerick University Press, 1995.
97 Monod, P.K., *Jacobitism and the English People, 1688–1788*, Cambridge University Press, 1989.
98 Moody, T.W., Martin, F.X. and Byrne, F.J. (eds), *A New History of Ireland*, vol. III, 1534–1689, Oxford University Press, 1976.
99 Nenner, H., 'Constitutional uncertainty and the Declaration of Rights' in B.C. Malament (ed.), *After the Reformation: Essays in Honor of J.H. Hexter*, Manchester University Press, 1980.
100 O'Brien, P. and Hunt, P., 'The Rise of a Fiscal State in England, 1485–1815', *Historical Research*, vol. LXVI, 1993.
101 Ogg, D., *England in the Reigns of James II and William III*, Oxford University Press, 1955.
102 Owen, J.B., *The Rise of the Pelhams*, Methuen, 1957.
103 Plumb, J.H., *The Growth of Political Stability in England, 1675–1725*, Macmillan, 1967.
104 Porter, R., *English Society in the Eighteenth Century*, Penguin, 1982.
105 Reitan, E.A., 'From Revenue to Civil List, 1689–1702', *Historical Journal*, vol. XIII, 1970.

106 Riley, P.W.J., *The Union of England and Scotland*, Manchester University Press, 1979.

107 Roberts, C., 'The Constitutional Significance of the Financial Settlement of 1690,' *Historical Journal*, vol. XX, 1977.

108 Roseveare, H., *The Financial Revolution, 1660–1760*, Longman, 1991.

109 Roseveare, H., *The Treasury: The Evolution of a British Institution*, Allen Lane, 1969.

110 Schwoerer, L.G., *The Declaration of Rights, 1689*, Johns Hopkins University Press, 1981.

111 Schwoerer, L.G. (ed.), *The Revolution of 1688–9: Changing Perspectives*, Cambridge, 1992.

112 Sharpe, J.A., *Crime in Early Modern England, 1550–1750*, Longman, 1984.

113 Shoemaker, R.B., *Prosecution and Punishment: Petty Crime and the Law in London and Rural Middlesex, c.1660–1725*, Cambridge University Press, 1991.

114 Simms, J.G., *Jacobite Ireland 1685–91*, Routledge & Kegan Paul, 1969.

115 Speck, W.A., *Reluctant Revolutionaries: Englishmen and the Revolution of 1688*, Oxford University Press, 1988.

116 Speck, W.A., *Tory and Whig: The Struggle in the Constituencies, 1701–15*, Macmillan, 1970.

117 Spurr, J., 'The Church of England, Comprehension and the Toleration Act of 1689', *English Historical Review*, vol. CIV, 1989.

118 Spurr, J., *The Restoration Church of England, 1646–89*, Yale University Press, 1991.

119 Stone, L. (ed.), *An Imperial State at War: Britain from 1689 to 1815*, Routledge, 1994.

120 Sykes, N., *Church and State in England in the Eighteenth Century*, Cambridge University Press, 1934.

121 Thomas, R., 'Comprehension and Indulgence', in G.F. Nuttall and 0. Chadwick (eds), *From Uniformity to Unity, 1662–1962*, SPCK, 1962.

122 Thompson, E.P., 'Eighteenth-century English Society: Class Struggle without Class', *Social History*, 1978.

123 Thompson, E.P., *Whigs and Hunters: The Origins of the Black Act*, Allen Lane, 1975.

124 Tomlinson, H., *Guns and Government: The Ordnance Office Under the Later Stuarts*, Royal Historical Society, 1979.

125 Walsh, J., Haydon, C. and Taylor, S. (eds), *The Church of England, c. 1689–c.1833: From Toleration to Tractarianism*, Cambridge University Press, 1993.

126 Watts, M., *The Dissenters from the Reformation to the French Revolution*, Oxford University Press, 1978.

127 Whatley, C., 'England, Scotland and the "Golden Ball": the Union of 1707', *The Historian*, no. 51, 1996.

128 Wilson, K., *The Sense of the People: Politics, Culture and Imperialism in England, 1715–85*, Cambridge University Press, 1995.
129 Wrightson, K. and Levine, D., *Poverty and Piety in an English Village: Terling, 1525–1700*, Academic Press, 1979.

ADDITIONAL MATERIAL

130 Bramston, Sir J., *Autobiography*, ed. Lord Braybrooke, Camden Society, 1845.
131 *Commons Journals*, Vol X.
132 Earle, P., *The World of Defoe*, Weidenfeld, 1976.
133 *Historical Manuscripts Commission, Dartmouth MSS*, Vol I.
134 *Historical Manuscripts Commission, House of Lords 1689–90.*
135 Locke, J., *Correspondence*, ed. E.S. de Beer, 8 vols, Oxford, 1976–89.
136 Nottingham University Library, MS PwA 2171.
137 Nottingham University Library, MS PwA 1330.
138 Trevelyan, G.M., *The English Revolution, 1688–9*, Oxford, 1938.

INDEX